GRAND KEY OF SOLOMON THE KING

ANCIENT HANDBOOK OF ANGEL MAGIC & DJINN SUMMONING

Pseudo Asaph Ben Berechiah

Ishtar Publishing
Vancouver

Grand Key of Solomon the King: Ancient Handbook of Angel Magic and Djinn Summoning

AN ISHTAR PUBLISHING BOOK:
978-1-926667-11-9

PRINTING HISTORY
Ishtar Publishing edition published 2009
1 3 5 7 9 10 8 6 4 2

Ishtar Publishing
141-6200 McKay Ave
Suite 716
Burnaby, BC
Canada V5H4M9

www.ishtarpublishing.com
Printed and bound in the United States.

TABLE OF CONTENTS

Chapters	Pages

Chapters	Pages

Chapters	Pages

Chapters	Pages

Ishtar Publishing's
Other Books Of Interest

Available

Book of Deady Names As Revealed To King Solomon By Jinn King Fiqitush

Coming Soon

Red Magic: Grimoire of Djinn Spells and Sorceries

Jinn Summoning: Compendium of Magical Evocations For Advanced Wizards

Al-Toukhi's Grimoire of Harut and Marut

In the name of God, Most Merciful and Compassionate

To commence: You have been asking me to write a book for you, comprised of benefits laid out sequentially. I thought I would assist you toward the means by which the People of Truth give guidence to others using source documents. I have summarized these, so that anyone who reads them can quickly grasp them.

First, I shall begin with what is reliable and a source of guidance, so that its reader may be safe from sources of criticism among the Scholars of Truth, who long for the spiritual science and adhere to the rules of Sacred Law, so that entreaty to the Creator, Glorious and Exalted, may come about.

I have explained what our predecessors spoke and concealed from the secrets of the scholars concerning the one- and two-part non-Arabic names and the like, such as the three-part names written in foreign tongues. I have transliterated these into Arabic so that they may be easy for their reader and that he may be safe from error.

Know: The prophet Moses was in a state of love known to the elect, where he gave up food and water and voluntarily feared God and wept. He would speak the Names until the term appointed by his Lord Most High was completed. On hearing what pertained to them of such names, the angels would descend to him out of every heaven with their exalted ranks. Thereupon he would say, "My need is with the Creator of the earth and the heavens," and recite the Most Beautiful Names and the Supreme Words, which neither earth nor heaven can withstand hearing, and which are the father of the world and all of creation.

I shall discuss each name, the angels associated with it, and the conjurations it requires, starting with the angels encompassing the Throne and the Footstool, the angels encircling the Canopies of Greatness and Glory, the angels enveloping the Pen and the Tablet, the angels who glorify God in the Inhabited House, the angel Isrāfīl [إسرافيل], who stands on the right hand of power, the intimate angel Jibrā'īl [جبرائيل], who stands on the left hand of power, the angel Mīkā'īl [ميكائيل], 'Izrā'īl [عزرائيل], the cherubim and the angels in charge of the spirits.

I shall explain this in its proper place, God Most High willing, so that the divine reward contained therein may be easy for its reader to earn, thus enabling him to rise to the highest degree and perceive the world of the heavenly realm. But it is the Divine who will guide to what is correct and who will assist with what each chapter brings. I shall elaborate on the non-Arabic words and the diacritical marks of the letters based on the best source. For whatever knowledge I am unfamiliar with, I will rely on what is recorded and established.

Following the discussion of those angels, I will mention the names that God Most High taught the prophet Moses, and the names by which the Divine raised Elias to a high place. After these are the names which Joshua the son of Nun spoke, whereupon the sun stood still for him and which Moses said to Og the son of Anak causing him to become bewildered, until Moses killed him.

Next come the names by which the celestial and terrestrial spirits are made to manifest, as well as names known as the Names of Tijan. By these, any of celestial or terrestrial Ruhaniyyah you wish to summon will answer out of obedience to God Most Great (the *ruhani* you summon will not be able to stay away from you for a single moment, even if he is in the remotest part of the east and you are in the remotest part of the west). Last are the names by which the Divine created each of the seven firmaments.

In addition, I will mention the seal of the angel Mīṭaṭrūn [ميططرون] (peace be upon him), its conjurations, its obedience, its uses, and instructions on how to use it (God willing, his will be the first seal to be discussed), as well as the Supreme Conjuration for all spirits.

Then I will give the seal of the angel Ruqayā'īl [رقيائيل] and its conjuration, its inscription, its uses, its rules and instructions on how to use it. I will show the seal of the terrestrial king Madhhab [مذهب] and what pertains to it, as is mentioned elsewhere.

Next, I will give the seal of Jibrā'īl [جبرائيل] (peace be upon him) and what pertains to it, as I did for others. After that, I will examine the seal of the terrestrial king Abya' [أبيض], and then the seal of the angel Samsamā'īl [سمسمائيل] and what pertains to it, as I did for the rest.

Furthermore, I will consider the seal of the angel Mīkā'īl [ميكائيل] (peace be upon him) and what pertains to it of instructions, important explanations, and conjurations that have been related concerning what benefits humankind.

Additionally, I will cover the seal of the angel Ṣarfayā'īl [صرفيائيل] (peace be upon him) and his great benefits, as well as a conjuration for the flying spirits of the air and their compliance. Next I will talk about Shamhūrash [شمهورش], his conjurations, and the quickness of his compliance, likewise Zawba'ah [زوبعة], his seal, and the greatness of his compliance. Then I will reveal instructions for the seal of the angel 'Anyā'īl [عنيائيل] and the excellence of his compliance. The Conjuration of the Regions as extracted from the books of mysteries follows, as well as the seal of Maymūn [ميمون] and what benefits and

fear it holds (**those are all seven seals**).

Then I will show you the seal of the Twelve Who Know the Secrets of Humankind and the rites and considerations pertaining to them. I will give instructions for the seal of Mahākīl [مهاكيل] **and Ṣakhr ibn ʻAmrū ibn Sarjīl ibn al-Abya' ibn Jamlīt** [صخر بن عمرو بن سرجيل بن الأبيض بن جمليت]. **I will mention the Aides and all that pertains to them. I will indicate the *mandal* of Solomon** (**peace be upon him**), **what pertains to it, its guardian Mahākīl** [مهاكيل], **and its instructions and uses. Finally, I will give the names of seership, against which neither jinn nor human can transgrass. For Maymūn** [ميمون], **who responds for anything, I give the names on the handle** [**of the spear**], **prescribed for every afflicted person, and the names for slaying. Then I give the names of Abū al-Walid's** [أبو الوليد] **knife, intended for every obstinate tyrant and rebellious demon**.

I shall then cite the seals of the Terrestrial Kings. They are: the seal of Khandash [خندش] **and Naykal** [نيكل] **and the instructions and rules pertaining to them; the seal of Abū Maʻbad Zunbūr** [أبو معبد زنبور], **its instructions, its uses, and its commetary; the seal of Maymūn Abū Nūkh** [ميمون أبو نوخ], **his compliance, and the excellence of his obedience; the seal of Aḥmar the Koreishite** [الأحمر القرشي], **who is prepared to do anything; and the seal of Ḥāminah** [حامنه], **its instructions, its Aides, its uses, its specialty, the quickness of compliance, and its mighty protection. I shall keep**

any explanation in the chapters following these brief, until their place of discussion comes. God Most High willing, what I have compiled will suffice.

I shall discuss the names on the Pentacle of Solomon (peace be upon him), which is the great Altar upon which he had the spirits swear a covenant, and on which Jibrā'īl [جبرائيل], Mīkā'īl [ميكائيل], Isrāfīl [إسرافيل], and 'Azrā'īl [عزرائيل] sat, on the day they swore that covenant, as well as its instructions, its guardians, its uses, and the words and rites to employ.

You will learn the scorching names by which you torment the spirits, along with an accurate commentary on the purpose of their utilization. I will mention the secrets lodged at every chosen station. Then I will discuss the Carpet and its commentary, the Perfect Names, the Twelve Names and the manner of attaining Elias's knowledge.

Finally, I shall discuss Simia (dark alchemy), by which one can make the blind to see, along with its bewildering, wondrous, and sublime states, topics, and types. The highest grades extant of these are those whose gains bring nearer pursuits whose gifts are noble. These elevated he who was elevated and caused lights to appear on a dark night, and brought near what he wished to be near, even if it was far, and sent afar what he wished to be far, even if it was near. Additionally, if he so wished, he could produce

all the various metals of the earth, fires from which fire cannot, through any physical act, be obtained, and so on, all by the power of the Lord, the King, the Bestower, He who dispatches the winds to the clouds. (Glory be to Him besides whom there is no god!) One can gain insight into that only by success through the Divine and by the blessing of His names.

Names Of Power To Awaken The Throne Bearers

In the name of God, Almighty and Great. The first in order of submission are the Throne-bearers, and the names by which they obey are:

Bihamyafaḥ [بهميفح], **Bijammah** [بجمة], **Yaghfir** [يغفر], **Mayhaqar** [ميهقر], **Masīl** [مسيل], **Shahūn** [شهون], **Shahūn** [شهون], **Bijahoon** [بجاهون], **Malayhoon** [مليهون].

Explanation: O Lord, You are the One; You are

the Ultimate; You are the Omnipotent; You are the Living, the Ever Subsistent, the Lord of all things, the God of all things, the Knower of all things, the Omnipotent over all things. Not an atom's weight escapes Your knowledge. You are transcendent and therefore cannot be seen.

Know, may God support you, that if you say these names with cleanliness of body, clothes, and surroundings, and with a sincere heart, angels of light will descend to you, and the heavens, the earth, everything in them, and everything between them will tremble. You can use these names for inciting spirits, entering the presence of sovereigns, acceptance, binding tongues, marriage proposals, the fulfillment of needs, summoning celestial Ruhaniyyah, protection, healing and reproval in pursuit of the approval of the Lord Most High.

Names Of Power On The Rod Of Moses

The second speech is that by which the Divine created the angels of the Canopies of Greatness and Glory. It is these names that Adam (peace be upon him) said, where-

upon God accepted his repentance. Moreover, they are the ones with which Jesus the son of Mary (peace be upon him) resurrected the dead and cured the living; he would say them over ailments and they would be cured by the permission of the Lord. If you say them in a state of cleanliness, the mountains will tremble from their greatness. They are as follows:

‘Anī [عنى], **Bayrakh** [بيرخ], **Bayrūkh** [بيروخ], **Barkhawā** [برخوا], **Shayrakh** [شيرخ], **Shārūkh** [شاروخ], **Yatmakh** [يتمخ], **Shakhāyā** [شخايا], **Mūkh** [موخ], **Fāsikh** [فاسخ], **Shamūkh** [شموخ], **Shamīkhā** [شميخا], **Makhīkhā** [مخيخا], **Arīkhā** [أريخا], **Bayrūkhā** [بيروخا], **Bihayā** [بهيا], **Ya Būma** [يا بوما], **Hūriyāwamaḥ** [هورياومح], **Maharūt** [مهاروت], **Ya Hūh** [هوه يا], **Shaymū** [شيمو], **Malsayāmīm** [ملسياميم], **Maqnānā** [مقنانا], **Bishafharaz** [بشفهرز], **Harāzir** [هرازر], **Bārūkh** [باروخ], **Sharfayūkh** [شرفيوخ], **Bālūkhā** [بالوخا]. **You are the Originator of the heavens and the earth.**

In addition to the names, these characters were on the rod of Moses (peace be upon him):

لبهايم وبربتيا يا عزيز ى م مح 6 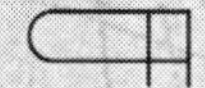 ال مح 8 ٢ ٣ ١ ال

له غ ح كا تباع ابى رعم رص ع ن ماع د سدى ع ع ماع له

Explanation: You are the Creator, besides whom there is no god, the most glorious of those who are remembered, the most entitled to be worshipped, the most worthy of being praised, the most generous of those who are asked, and the most bountiful of those who give. There

is no god but You, the most knowledgeable of those who know, the wisest of those who rule, the most helpful of those from whom help is sought. There is no god but You. You are hidden from creation. You have ascribed kindness unto Yourself. You alone possess the most beautiful names. You encompass all things in knowledge and power. When invoked, You answer. When asked, You give. You have recorded traces and reckoned life spans. You are the King, the Overpowering, the One, the Triumphant. There is no god save You. You abase with Your power and elevate by Your might whom You will. You are God, the Master. The hearts of all creatures are in Your hand, and You can turn them as You please. Speech is what You have spoken; decree, what You have decreed; judgment, what You have judged. No one can repulse Your command, nor can anyone rescind Your determination. You are the Living, the Ever Subsistent.

Know, my brother, that these names are scattered over the rod of Moses (peace be upon him). They are thirty-one names—ten on each side. Among them is a name by which one can perform miracles, open locks, break spells, bind tongues, divide evildoers, subdue tyrants, and summon any terrestrial spirit. You can employ them for abduction, reproval, separation, love, arousal, bringing those who are away, and fulfilling all needs, by the power of the Lord Most High. You can use them for all righteous deeds.

Among their wondrous properties is that, if you inscribe them on an Indian mirror and set it out

under the stars for seven days in the manner that will, God Most High willing, be described later, any spirit you summon will answer—not one of them will fail to come to you. You can also use them for finding stolen and hidden items. When you say them, angels will descend to you, each having two wings—one spanning the east and the other the west—and they can summon any of the Spiritual Kings you wish. They have sundry other usages.

Names Of Power To Awaken The Angels Of Mercy

These names are associated with the Angels of Mercy, who are obliged to obey them. The name of the angel in charge of them is Isrāfīl [إسرافيل] **(peace be upon him), on whose forehead these names are written, and who stands on the right hand of power, awaiting the command to sound the trumpet, by which the souls will be gathered. These are the names:**

Thahīth [ثهيث], **Mātīt** [ماتيت], **Samāsamā** [سماسما], **Saymīmā** [سيميما], **Batāyā** [بتايا], **Yamaqyā** [يمقيا], **Hāṭūl** [هاطول], **Yamūkh** [يموخ], **Hūh** [هوه], **Māyakhūkh** [مايخوخ]

Explanation: You are the Powerful—where are those who are powerful? You are the Glorious—where are those who are glorious? You are the Living, the Ever Subsistent. Answer, O company of Aides, by the leave of the Divine.

Know, my friend, that if you say these purified names, the earth and the mountains will tremble from their greatness, and all the spirits of the angels, spirits, and jinn will hurry to you. These are white angels holding banners of white light.

The names are also the names of bewilderment. If you utter them against a tyrant, he will become bewildered and unable to speak. The same applies to every adversary, envier, and transgressor. By the permission of God Most High, you can use them for binding tongues, protection, and against all harmful diseases. None of the angels in charge of the regions of the earth will fail to come to you. Further, you must neither utter them, except in a state of cleanliness, nor employ them, except for that of which the Lord Most High approves.

Names Of Power On The Forehead Of The Angel Gabriel

This part pertains to the names written on the forehead of Jibrā'īl [جبرائيل] (peace be upon him), who stands on the right hand of power, awaiting the command to deliver divine inspiration. Obedience to them is incumbent upon the angels associated with the Tablet comprising knowledge of all things and the Exalted Knowledge. When you summon them thereby, they will answer out of obedience to the Divine, Mighty and Majestic. With His names and these names, He created them. Moreover, they are written on the forehead of Jibrā'īl [جبرائيل] (peace be upon him), and are the ones Jesus the son of Mary (peace be upon him) would say on important occasions. They are as follows:

Ṭash [طش], Ṭash [طش], Ṭashaṭ [طشط], Ṭashah [طشه], Yūhanīṭ [يو هنيط], Hūmiyāṭ [هو مياط], Hūthāwuṭ [هو ثاوط]. Glorious is God, Mighty and Majestic, and He has power over all things.

Explanation: Glory be unto You, O Living One. Glory be unto You, O Ever Subsistent One. Glory be unto You, O Reliance. Glory be unto You, O He who neither begot nor was begotten, and whom there was none like. There is no god save You, none omnipotent save You, and none worthy of worship save You.

Obedience to them is incumbent upon all the angels. When you summon them thereby, they will respond. You can employ them in piousness and righteousness.

Seven Names Taught To the Angel Michael

There are seven names that the Lord Most High taught Mīkā'īl [ميكائيل] (peace be upon him), and with which he and all the angels in the seventh heaven standing between the Tablet and the Throne glorify God. Angels of light serve them. They are the angels who give succor to all the prophets. In their hands are spears of light that burst in flames at disobedient spiri-

tual and terrestrial angels. Whenever you summon them thereby, they will answer. You can use them for all pious and righteous works and for summoning the Thaqufat [angelic overseers of the seasons] who are in the regions of the earth. These are the pure, noble, purified names written on the forehead of Mīkā'īl [ميكائيل] **(peace be upon him)**:

Shahā [شها], **Shawīn** [شوين], **Kanūfash** [كنوفش], **Lūnīm** [لونيم], **Kaylīm** [كيليم], **Ya'ṭīsh** [يعطيش], **Bālah** [باله].

Explanation: **Glory be unto You, O God, O Overpowering One. Glory be unto You, O Lord, O Subduer. Glory be unto You, O He who knows of the fall of a leaf from a tree. Glory be unto You, O He who is clothed with majesty and dignity. Glory be unto You, O He who has reckoned every life span. You, my Lord, are exalted far above what the oppressors say**.

Know, may the Creator give you success that, if you say them, angels of light on horses of light, holding swords of light, will descend to you. They are the masters of stabbing and you can put them to use for reproval, healing, protection, burning, abduction, binding tongues, and inciting the spiritual and terrestrial angels. You can employ them for all things by the permission of God Most High.

Seven Names Taught To The Angel Azrael

There are seven names, by which the Lord Most High taught the angel ʻAzrāʼīl [عزرائيل] to seize souls. These are the names:

Kashlaʻ [كشلع], **Yaʻlas** [يعلس], **Yaʻkalam** [يعكلم], **Shatīkāl** [شتيكال], **Jamaʻahum** [جمعهم], **Makāy** [مكاي], **Kalwā** [كلوا].

Explanation: I am the Creator. I am the Maker. I am the Originator. I am the Restorer. I do as I please. I am the Giver of Life and the Giver of Death. I am the Overpowering, the Majestic. I am the Oft-forgiving, Who alone possesses mercy. Come forth, O soul, out of obedience unto the command of God.

Know, may the Divine support you, that these are the most sublime of the Seven Canopies. Those of exalted constitution and the glory encompassing all things will follow them. Obedience to them is incumbent upon all celestial bodies and all the spiritual angels who glorify God therein.

Know that these names are names of bewilderment: when you enter the presence of a tyrannical sovereign, an adversary you wish to suppress, or an envier whose plot you wish to return upon his own head, say those names and he will become bewildered and unable to speak. However, do not say them except on important occasions. They can likewise stun all celestial and terrestrial spirits and, by the permission of the Lord Most High, are useful for binding tongues, entering the presence of sovereigns, discovering hidden things in dreams, covenanting with the Spiritual Kings, enquiring about unseen affairs throughout the world, making pacts with the Kings, the mightiest shield, and the greatest flame.

Names Of Power For The Seventh Heaven

Here are seven pure names, and with them the Divine One created the devastating angels of the seventh Heaven. No earth or heaven can bear hearing them. If you recite them in a clean space, angels on horses of flames, holding green banners, willing to comply with your

every demand, will descend to you out of obedience to the names of God Most High. Utter them only for that of which the Lord, Mighty and Majestic, approves. Moreover, these are the names that Adam (peace be upon him) said, whereupon God forgave him. They are as follows:

Bakhṭā [بخطا], **Sayṭā** [صيطا], **'Ajā** [عجا], **Elyon**, **Hānīt** [هانيط], **Sam'ā**, [سمعا], **Sha'aytā** [شعيتا].

Explanation: Glory be unto You, O Liberator of Necks. Glory be unto You, O Causer of Causes. Glory be unto You, O Revealer of the Book. Glory be unto You, O Generous One, O Bestower. Glory be unto You, O Living One who dies not. Glory be unto You, O my God and God of humanity. You created me, my Lord, by Your hand, and preferred me unto many of Your creatures. Therefore unto You belong praise, grace, power, and blessings. Blessed and exalted are You, our Lord. I ask Your forgiveness and repent unto You.

You can employ them, by the permission of God Most High, for any pious act you wish—anything the Lord approves of—such as protection, healing, reproval, subdual, abduction, covenanting, and inciting the Spiritual and Terrestrial Kings. Obedience to them is incumbent upon them. Whenever you summon them therewith, they will answer.

Names Of Power For The Sixth Heaven

These are twenty names of the Divine, Mighty and Majestic, which they serve with obedience and compliance. If you say them, angels on green horses, each angel wearing different colored clothing, holding swords of light, will descend to you. They are the greatest flame. You can use them for anything. They are the interlocutors concerning humiliation and disfiguration. These are their names:

Haflas [هفلس], **Saṭi‘** [سطيع], **Shaklaman** [شكلمن], **‘Alayt** [عليت], **Hash** [هش], **Kahlaḥ** [كهلح], **Ayjī‘** [ايجيع], **Ayshaṭīn** [ايشطين], **‘Alsīm** [علسيم], **Ṣalṣā** [صلصا], **Ṣalī‘** [صليع], **Ḥajīl** [حجيل], **Ta‘līsh** [تعليش], **Ṭīṭ** [طيط], **Shak-halaj** [شكهلج], **‘Alsayfāṭ** [علسيفاط], **Alkhahīlānīṭ** [الخهيلانيط], **Haykal** [هيكل], **Malīkh** [مليخ], **Haṭal** [هطل], **Hayṭal** [هيطل].

Explanation: Glory be unto You, O possessor of sovereignty and might. Glory be unto You, O possessor of power and force. Glory be unto You, O Living One who dies not. Glory be unto You, O He who is transcendent and too subtle to be

seen. Glory be unto You, O He unto whom belong the sovereignty of this world and the world to come. Exalted are You, my Lord, far above what the oppressors say.

Know, my friend—may the Lord give you success—that if you say them in a state of cleanliness, the mountains and the earth will shake from their greatness. You can use them, by the permission of God Most High, for reproval, degredation, abduction, slitting, protection, and questioning the Ruhaniyyah and the Servants on any day. Whenever you summon them thereby, they will answer out of obedience to the Lord Most High and to His names.

Names Of Power For The Fifth Heaven

There are twelve names of God Most High, which He taught Moses (peace be on him), who supplicated Him with them, whereupon He answered his supplication. They are as follows:

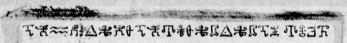

Sāh [ساه], Asāsūd [اساسود], Adsā [ادسا], Adonai, Badi' [بديع], 'Ajīj [عجيج], Halīfī'ā [هليفيعا], Yanfī'ā [ينفيعا], Salyā [سليا], Sa'āyāhū [سعاياهو], Saymīmā [سيميما], Yarūkh [يروخ], Sharnabūkh [شرنبوخ], Yā Lūkhā [يا لوخا].

Explanation: You, You, O Merciful One, O Compassionate One, O He of exalted status, O He who is worshipped at all times and in all ages, O He who is sacred everywhere, O He who is glorified in all languages, O Magnificent One, O Sovereign One, O He of infinite beneficence, O He of eternal grace, pardon Your sinful servant. Grant me deliverance and hear me, O Glorious One. Answer my supplication, O One, through Your greatness. Verily You are powerful over all things.

Another Explanation: O Merciful One, O Compassionate One, O Beneficent One, grant me deliverance and hear me. O Glorious One, answer my supplication. O Almighty One, forgive me. O One, there is no god save You. You are my Lord and the Lord of all things. I ask Your forgiveness and repent unto You.

Know, my friend, that these names are majestic, pure, and purified, and you can employ them for all pious actions, summoning the Spiritual Kings, conjurations, reproval, subjugation, protection, and healing. Out of obedience to them, none whom you summon will fail to come. Among their special wonders is that when you supplicate the Lord Most High for something thereby, He will answer you and fulfill your need. They are also for love, arousal and har-

mony between two conflicting parties, binding tongues, fulfilling needs, gettng information about the unseen through dreams, entering the presence of sovereigns, revelation through the mirror, marriage proposals, and trade. You can use them for anything.

Names Of Power For The Fourth Heaven

Whenever you summon them thereby, they will answer with obedience and compliance. They are the angels in charge of those who record deeds, and the angels in charge of the children of Adam. These are their majestic names:

Tayfāb [تيفاب], **Sayfāb** [سيفاب], **Shaylūb** [شيلوب], **Haylūb** [هيلوب], **Saṭūb** [سطوب], **Hatūb** [هطوب], **Tayfūb** [تيفوب], **Ṭāṭūb** [طاطوب], **Ṭūb** [طوب]. **There is no power and no strength save with God , Exalted and Magnificent.**

Explanation: Glory be unto You, O Lord of Lords. Glory be unto You, O Liberator of Necks. Glory

be unto You, O Cause of Causes. Glory be unto You, O Opener of Doors. Glory be unto You, O Oft-pardoning One, O Oft-forgiving One. Glory be unto You, O Quick One, O Bestower. Glory be unto You, O Revealer of the Book. My Lord, my Lord, my Lord, subordinate Your servants unto me.

Know, may the Creator guide you, that you can employ them for righteous works and prosperous matters—for entering the presence of sovereigns, the fulfillment of needs, silencing, acceptance, supplication in prayers, and inciting the celestial and terrestrial Kings. They will be useful, by the permission of God Most High, for anything you desire.

Names Of Power For The Third Heaven

Such are the names by which the Divine raised Enoch to a high place. They are these: Kaṭayūrash [كطيورش], Hīl [هيل], Ṭāyaṭar [طايطر], Malayhar [مليهر], Lawaytam [لويتم], Barkaylam [بركيلم], Ehieh. You are my Lord.

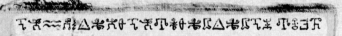

Explanation: Glory be unto You, O He who is great in power and subdues His servants by death. Glory be unto you, O He who is filled with glory. Glory be unto You, O He whose glory fills the earth and the heavens. Glory be unto You, O He unto whom belong thanks and praise. Glory be unto You, O He unto whom belong immortality and everlastingness. Glory be unto You, O He unto whom belong might and grace. Glory be unto You, O He unto whom belong the most beautiful names. My Lord, I am weak, so strengthen me; base, so exalt me; needy, so give me of the treasures of Your mercy.

Know, may God Most High guide you, that the angels of the third Heaven must obey these noble names. Whenever you summon them thereby, they will obediently comply with any considerable task you wish; the Lord Most High willing, not one of them will fail to come to you. You can use them for all things. When angels of light holding spears of light descend to you, they will help you and render you victorious over tasks, great and small, that are difficult for you. If you utter them against a tyrant, they will annihilate him, or against an adversary, strike him dumb, provided you are in the previously described, stipulated state. By the permission of God Most High, you can employ them for protection, separation, burning, conjuration, abduction, and seeking revelation from any spirit.

Names Of Power For The Second Heaven

The inhabitants of the second Heaven must obey these. Whenever you summon them thereby, they will answer out of obedience to the names of the Lord Most High. They are these:

Bakhamlīth [بخمليث], **Shalkhīthā** [شلخيثا], **Malkhīthā** [ملخيثا], **Beshaṭaṭ** [بشطط], **Makakh** [مكخ], **Alālahīq** [الالهيق], **Yāh** [يه], **Yāmanah** [يامنه], **Hayuwā** [هيوا], **Hayuhā** [هيها], **Ḥakmīkh** [حكميخ], **Khajaj** [خجج], **Ṭakh** [طخ], **Ṭakh** [طخ].

Explanation: Glory be unto You, O God, O Resurrecter. Glory be unto You, O Lord, O Inheritor. Glory be unto You, O Divine One, O Loving One. Glory be to You, O Creator, O Glorious One. Glory be unto You, O He of overwhelming force. My Lord, expand my chest, make my affair easy for me, and give me a helping authority from Your presence.

Know, my brother—may the Lord guide you towards ease and goodness—that obedience to these majestic, pure, and purified names is incumbent upon the angels of the second Heaven. Whenever you summon them thereby, they will answer and hasten out of obedience to the Divine, Mighty and Majestic, and to His glorious names, provided you are in the previously stipulated state. You can employ them for everything. They possess the sword that subdues the inhabitants of the seven Heavens. You can employ them for reproval, healing, burning, and killing. No matter what you need, not one of them will fail to come. By God Most Great, I ask you, my friend, to employ them only in obedience to the Lord, Mighty and Majestic.

Names Of Power For The First Heaven

The angels of the first Heaven glorify Him by these names. If you say them while in the previously described state, angels holding blazing torches that burn whoever dis-

obeys God Most High, will come to you. These names are as follows:

Yūh [يوه], **Yūh** [يوه], **Yāhū** [ياهو], **Hayūh** [هيوه], **Yā Shayrakhanj** [يا شيرخنج], **Yā Shīlamakhūt** [يا شيلمغوت], **'Awayālikh** [عويالخ], **Hūh** [هوه], **Shaymūtā** [شيموتا], **Hīkh** [هيخ]. **You, You hold this power.**

Explanation: You are First; therefore, there is nothing before You. You are Last; therefore, there is nothing after You. You are Pure; therefore, nothing is like unto You. You are Hidden; therefore, nothing can perceive You. You are the One without increase. You are the Subduer without aide, the Director without consultant and the Owner of Sovereignty. You give sovereignty unto whomever You will and take away sovereignty from whomever You will. You exalt whomever You will and abase whomever You will. In Your hand is goodness. Indeed, You have power over all things.

Know, my friend, that these magnificent, noble, purified names are the greatest names. If you say them, a flame of fire will exit your heart without your perceiving it, if you are in the previously described state. Thereby, all the Ruhaniyyah of the regions will obey you. They are for the unveiling of the Spirits of Conjuration and for tasks both great and small. They empower over all the Ruḥaniyyah of the Angels of Conjuration. You can employ them for all things, even for entering the presence of sovereigns and restraining any stubborn tyrant or demon.

By the grace of God Most High, this completes the seven Heavens.

Names Of Power For The Seventh Firmament (Sun)

The Lord, Mighty and Majestic used twenty of His names to create the angels of the seventh firmament, who glorify Him by them. They must obey them. Whenever you summon them thereby, they will answer. They are these sublime, blessed, noble, magnificent names, which produce a great obedience and a profound proof:

Qaṣiṣ [قصيص], **Mabṭayūb** [مبطيوب], **'Ajmakal** [عجمكل], **Hayhayawā** [هيهيوا], **Ṭaṭah** [ططه], **Yaṭaṭiyah** [يططيه], **Iyyāk** [إياك], **Lū'** [لوض], **Ḥafaṣ** [حفص], **Hadhāl** [هذال], **Hajam** [حجم], **Hasā** [هسا], **Bajaḥaṭ** [بجحط], **Haytoot** [هيتوت], **Ṣafratan** [صفرتن], **Ṭayhayāl** [طيهيال], **Hafūh** [هفوه], **Taḥkum** [تحكم], **Hayhām** [هيهام], **Hayhām** [هيهام].

Explanation: Glory be unto You, O He of exalted status. Glory be unto You, O He of infinite beneficence. Glory be unto You, O He who is glorified

in every language. Glory be unto You, O He who is hallowed everywhere. Glory be unto You, O He who is worshipped everywhere. Glory be unto You, O He of abiding grace. You are Exalted, my Lord, far above what the oppressors say.

Know, my friend—may God Most High give you success—that these honorable, benign, glorious, pure, purified names are the ones Joshua the son of Nun (peace be upon him) said on Tuesday, whereupon the sun moved backwards. Moses (peace be upon him) uttered them against Og the son of Anak, who became bewildered, until Moses killed him. All the angels of the seventh firmament are obliged to obey them. Moses also said them to the king when he visited him; he took hold of the king's belt and spat into his mouth, whereupon he instantly collapsed by the permission of God Most High.

The Lord Most High willing, you can use them for binding tongues, entering the presence of sovereigns, fulfilling needs, restraining tyrants, and burning rebellious spirits. You can charge them with abasement and transfiguration, and can stun subordinate celestial angels.

If you say these names with sincerity and while in the previously described state, a flame of fire that will burn every spirit it encounters will issue forth from your mouth. Be careful not to say them while one of your Aides is with you, as he will suffer.

Additionally, as I mentioned before, do not say them unless you are somewhere clean. The chief angel in charge of them, out of obedience to the names of God Most High, will come to you, compliant with your command concerning all that you desire of the pleasure of the Lord, Mighty and Majestic. If you enter the presence of an oppressive, despotic king, the Divine will subject him to you. If you summon a king of the jinn therewith, he will come immediately, quicker than a flash of lightning. If you are uncertain about an Aide, then entreat therewith and say, "Bring me N., whether he is of the angels or the terrestrial Ruhaniyyah, and command him as I wish, out of obedience to the names of God Most High." If you fight an opponent, you will overcome him thereby. By the permission of the Lord Most High, you can use them for all acts of piety, great and small.

Names Of Power For The Sixth Firmament (Jupiter)

These are eleven names of the Creator, Mighty and Majestic. If you say them while in the previously described state, yellow angels holding yellow banners and yellow spears will come. When they speak, a flame of fire issues forth from their mouths out of anger towards those who disobey the Lord Most High. If you recite them over ailments, the permission of God Most High will cause their cure. The names are these:

Tadas [تدس], **Tabadūs** [تبدوس], **Tabdahūdas** [تبدهودس], **Waqas** [وقس], **Hamayṣ** [هميص], **Yamas** [يمس], **Qarqatās** [قرقتاس], **Yarahūdas** [يرهودس], **'Amdas** [عمدس], **Bālārqash** [بالارقش], **Hayṣūs** [هيصوس]. **Blessed is our Lord in His most exalted glory.**

Explanation: Glory be unto You, O One, O Unique One. Glory be unto You, O Singular One, O Ultimate One. Glory be unto You, O He who is above all things. Glory be unto You, O He who will resurrect all the dead. Glory be unto You, O He who rules and is clothed with majesty. Glory be unto You, O He who is great in power and praise. Glory be unto You, O He who subdues His servants by death and annihilation. I ask You through the magnificence of Your most beautiful names and most glorious words by which I have invoked You to subordinate unto me Your intimate angels and unseen spirits. Indeed, You are the Creator of the heavens and the earth, what is in them, and all the creatures between them, O Judge of the Day of Judgment, O God, O Lord of the Worlds.

Know, may the Lord guide you, that if these names are inscribed on a gold ring or on a green stone in gold, and a person with hemiplegia caused by Possessing Winds is brought to you, and you rub it against his face, it will cause his cure by the permission of God Most High. When you say them, the spirits in the earth and the heaven tremble. You can use the names, by the permission of the Lord Most High, for summoning major and minor spirits (not one of them will fail to come to you). They will be at your disposal out of obedience to the names of God Most High. Whenever you invoke the Lord Most High thereby regarding a need, He will fulfill it for you. Additionally, whenever you summon a King, he will appear before you out of obedience to the names of God Most High. Therefore guard the secrets of what I have imparted to you, and give them neither to those unworthy nor to those without religion or creed.

Know that you can perform any of the foregoing secrets only by purifying your heart for your Lord, making your intention sincere, entreaty to your Lord, humbling yourself before Him, appealing for aid, and working without compensation, just as He commanded you. There is no power or strength, save in the Creator, Exalted and Magnificent.

Names Of Power For The Fifth Firmament (Mars)

These are twenty names of God, Mighty and Majestic, by which the Divine created the angels of the fifth firmament. They must obey them. Whenever you summon them therewith, they will answer. When you are in the appropriate state—namely, favorable conditions in terms of food and drink, cleanliness, and sincerity of intention—angels of red light, holding spears of red light with red banners from east to west, will come to you; they are the Angels of Wrath. These are the names:

By Shamakh [بشمخ], **Alhārabā** [الهاربا], **Walāyalakh** [ولايلخ]. **Haste and come, O Yāṭawīkh** [ياطويغ], **Amyarāyikh** [اميرايخ], **Batūlā** [بتولا], **Abarūs** [ابروس], **Arbā** [اربا], **Wahdabīkh** [وهدبيغ], **Wadārī** [وداري], **Marūh**

[مروه], Dhardhawā [ذرذوا], Zararmahā [زررمها], Armayūṭiyā [ارميوطيا], Arat [ارت], Artātim [ارتاتم] . Hasten, Hasten, angels of my Lord. Hasten ye unto me by the right of these names with which the Lord created You.

Explanation: Glory be unto You, O He who is hidden from all of creation. Glory be unto You, Who is clothed with dignity and majesty. Glory be unto You, Who is the master of all of creation. Glory be unto You, Who is great in power and glory. Glory be unto You, Who is too exalted and subtle to be seen. Glory be unto You, Who knows what is in the seven highest firmaments. Glory be unto You, Who knows what is beneath the earth. Glorified and exalted are You, my Lord. There is no lord save You, no conqueror save You, and no rightful object of worship save You. I ask You, my Lord, to subject Your angels unto me, that I may seek their assistance in what You love and what pleases You.

Know, my friend, that the angels of the fifth firmament must obey these names with great obedience and quick compliance. Following are some of the wonders of their properties: If you wish a celestial or terrestrial spirit to appear, then go to a clean, pure, and furnished house fumigated with sweet-smelling incense, and bring with you a group of trustworthy and respected people to listen to the names of the Lord Most High. You recite the names twenty-one times and say, "Show ye me the angel N./the ruhani N./the ifreet N./the jinni clinging to the body of N." and he will appear for you, even if he is of the hidden spirits. Also, if you wish to kill a despotic king or rebellious ifreet, inscribe these names on a knife and set it out under the stars for seven days and nights. Thereafter, recite the names, write the names on the floor, insert the knife into any letter you wish, and order them to kill him and he will be killed, even if he is in the east and you are in the west. If a transgressive possessing jinni rebels against you, write the names in a glass bowl, wash them off with water, and sprinkle it on the possessed person's face and you will see a wonder by the permission of God Most High.

Names Of Power For The Fourth Firmament (Saturn)

These are thirty names of God, Mighty and Majestic, for obedience and compliance from the inhabitants of the fourth firmament. Whenever you summon them, they will answer; giant angels of light holding spears of fire will descend to you. Let not their appearance or authority frighten you. If you summon a King and he disobeys you, and you wish to control him, then summon him and he will come to

you out of obedience to the names of the Lord, Mighty and Majestic, even if he is in the seventh firmament. These names are the thirty Names of Tijan:

O Maṣqaṣ [مصقص], **O Khālīkhā** [خاليخا], **O Bārī** [باري], **O Lūtā** [لوتا], **O Sahyāl** [سهيال], **O Hūbāl** [هوبال], **O Lūhāyim** [لوهايم], **O Nūhīm** [نوهيم], **O Rakhbīlā** [رخبيلا], **O Lūshā** [لوشا], **O Darbīlā** [دربيلا], **O Rakhbīlā** [رخبيلا], **O Razbīlā** [رزبيلا], **O Najlātā** [نجلاتا], **O Qarnātā** [قرناتا], **O Dhabāl** [ذبال], **O Hūhiyah** [هوهيه], **Yāh** [ياه], **Rīyah** [ريه], **Hī** [هي], **O Shanūt** [شنوت], **O Sahalū'** [سهلوع], **O 'Ūhīm** [عوهيم], **Ṭaṭ** [طط], **Ṭaṭ** [طط], **Bakh** [بخ], **Bakh** [بخ], **Samā** [سما], **Samā** [سما], **Samā** [سما], **O Mūshī** [موشي], **O Mūshī** [موشي], **O Mūshī** [موشي]. **Peace to him who follows guidance.**

Explanation: Glory be unto You, O Most Merciful One. Glory be unto You, O He of exalted sovereignty. Glory be unto You, O He of infinite beneficence, O He of graceful pardon. Glory be unto You, O He of subtle kindness. Glory be unto You, O He of comprehensive forgiveness. Glory be unto You, O He who does not fear the lapse of time and therefore does not haste. Glory be unto You, O He who accepts the repentance of sinners. My Lord, expand my chest, make my affair easy for me, remove the impediment from my speech so that they may understand what I say, and give me a helping authority from Your presence. O object of every petition, You suffice me.

Know, may the Divine guide you, that the angels of the fourth firmament who traverse all the orbits glorify Him by these names. These are the Names of the Tijan. Thereby you can summon any of the spiritual or terrestrial Ruhaniyyah you wish and not one of them will fail to come to you. You can use them, by the permission of God Most High, for fulfilling needs, binding tongues, burning any spirit, bewildering any tyrant, and the manifestation of any spirit in any conjuration. Following are some of their specialties and wonders: If you write them somewhere, no jinn will enter that place, nor will a devil come near it. If you write them and hang them on a woman whose children are being killed by Stalker Jinn, who harrass her through her children, you will restrain them from her. If you write them and attach them to your arm, they will eliminate forgetfulness. If you write them and hang them on a child or someone who is confused, they will protect them from all ailments. (All of that is by the permission of God Most High.) If you write them in a cup for someone who has anger or misgivings, they will remove that by the permission of the Lord Most High.

Among their great wonders is that, if one prays to God Most High thereby for something He approves of, He will grant him it and answer his prayer. They have numerous uses, the mentioning of which would take long (they will be mentioned elsewhere).

Names Of Power For The Third Firmament (Venus)

God, Mighty and Majestic used these thirty of His names to create the angels of the third firmament and they use them to glorify God. Obedience to the names is obligatory to them. Whenever you summon the angels thereby, they will answer out of obedience to the Divine, Mighty and Majestic, and to His names. You can employ them, by the permission of God Most High, for inciting the spirits and anything you wish and of which the Lord Most Glorious approves. They are the following:

Ṭāsh [طاش], **Ṭashūsh** [طشوش], **Ṭāsh** [طاش], **Ṭash** [طش], **Ahyā** [اهيا], **Ahyāsh** [اهياش], **Hīsh** [هيش], **Hamā** [هما], **Hamāshāh** [هماشاه], **Shūsh** [شوش], **Yashmaṣa'** [يشمصع], **Ṭashūsh** [طشوش], **Ṭash** [طش], **Hayā** [هيا], **Hayā** [هيا], **Ṭarash** [طرش], **Yā Hāyāhā** [يا هاياها], **Sharah** [شره]. **Bajarah** [بجره], **Batashūsh** [بتشوش], **Hayhūsh** [هيهوش]. **Exalted is the Divine, the One, the Subduer. Answer me, O angels of my Lord.**

Explanation: Glory be unto You, O Possessor of Majesty and Generosity. Glory be unto You, O possessor of power and sovereignty. Glory be unto You, O possessor of favor and blessings. Glory be unto You, Who knows the secrets of all hearts. Glory be unto You, Who will gather all of creation on the Day of Resurrection.

Glory be unto You, Who has all things with Him in a hidden book. Glory be unto You, in Whose hand is every decreed matter. Exalted are You, my Lord, and therefore there is no rightful object of worship besides You, no conqueror besides You, and no omnipotent being besides You. By You, he who triumphs is made triumphant, and he who becomes powerful is made powerful. You are the Omnipotent, the Living, the Master of Majesty and Generosity.

Know, my friend—may the Divine guide you—that these names are a supreme shield and the greatest flame that can burn any spirit. With them, you can shield anyone you wish from celestial and terrestrial spirits, and you can shield people from all possessing jinn so they cannot possess them. Moreover, if you say them where sages are gathered, the names will burn their aides so they will have nothing to employ. If you wish to do that, then command your Aides to hold on under your garment where they will be safe from burning by your generosity; then you recite them. You can use them, by the permission of the Lord Most High, for many things, among them love, harmony, reconciliation between couples, the fulfillment of needs, and any real magic that is needed.

Furthermore, you can summon all kinds of spirits with them. Whenever you invoke them therewith, they will respond, obedient to the command of God, Exalted and Mighty and Majestic, and to His names. None of them will fail to come to you, provided you are in the previously described state, which consists of keeping clean in all situations, eating what is lawful, and restraining the tongue from superfluous speech. With that, the mirror will reveal the discovery of secrets to you; therewith you will learn of secret matters and other things, such as the evident sciences, and you can rid believing men and women of any affliction you wish.

Therefore, guard—I implore you by the Divine One, my friend—the preserved secret that has come to you and the profound wisdom that has reached you; clench it with both your hands; do not mock it or it will mock you; and use it for what pleases God Most High. Invoke the Creator and trust in Him—what an excellent trustee, what an excellent protector, and what an excellent helper is He!

Names Of Power For The Second Firmament (Mercury)

With these names, God Most High created the inhabitants of the second firmament, who glorify Him therewith, obey them and speak them. Whenever you summon them thereby, they will respond out of obedience to the Divine One, Mighty and Majestic, and to His noble, magnificent, majestic, pure, immaculate names. Thereby you can employ them for whatever you wish of what God approves of, provided you are in the previously described state, which includes sincerity, having a good opinion about others, compassion for God's creatures, exalting the glorious Creator above every imperfection, earnest entreaty to Him, appeal for His aid, and trust in Him. The names are as follows:

O God, the Mighty, the Wise, Amlī, [املي], **Makhrasā** [مخرسا], **Yabkhā** [يبخا], **Mareīthā** [مرتيثا], **Sakhāfay'ā** [سخافيعا], **Qabīkhā** [قبيخا], **Quddūs** [قدوس], **Quddūsā** [قدوسا], **Shalmīthā** [شلميثا], **Ḥayūm** [حيوم], **Qayyūmā** [قيوما], **Ay** [اى], **Yā Ḥannānā** [يا حنانا] , **Ḥānāniyā** [حانانيا],

Quddūs [قدوس], Qayyūm [قيوم], Aw [او], Yaẓlaman [يظلمن], Kasa' [كسع], Salsa' [سلسع], 'Āl [عال], Sa'laj [سعلج], Akh [اخ], Arādūnā [ارادونا], Samāsamā [سماسما]. Majestic are Your names. Holy is Your glory. Exalted is Your remembrance in Your heavens and Your earth, and all who are therein have surrendered unto Your greatness.

Explanation: Glory be unto You, O Originator. Glory be unto You, O Restorer. Glory be unto You, O He of the noble Throne. Glory be unto You, O He of overwhelming force. Glory be unto You, O He who does as He pleases. Glory be unto You, O annihilator of every obstinate tyrant.

Know, my friend—may the Lord support you—that these names are a secret of secrets and you can use them, by the permission of God Most High, for acts of piety such as harmony, the fulfillment of any need, entering the presence of sovereigns, the engagement of women, and calling down the spiritual and terrestrial Kings. The following are some of the wonders of their properties: If you write them on a parchment of deerskin or clean paper using saffron and musk dissolved in rose water, and place them under someone's head, they will give information of what will happen to that one, whether good or bad, throughout the person's whole year. If you inscribe them on a silver ring during a beneficent hour, they will protect its owner against all harm. If you write them on a clean dish, wash them off with clean water and sprinkle it on a possessed person's face, they will burn the pos-

sessing jinni. If any person speaks them in the approved manner mentioned, and blows on the face of a possessing jinni, the jinni will burn.

Names Of Power For The First Firmament (Moon)

With them God Most High created them. Whenever you summon them by these, they will answer heedfully and obediently. They have the angel Shadkhayā'īl [شدخيائيل] **(the angel Mīṭaṭrūn** [ميططرون]**) by the forelock, the angels who glorify in the firmament of the earth, and the supporters and helpers with the prophets. When you say the names, white and green angels of light holding spears of light, who incite all the angels under the firmament of the earth, and are in charge of the forelocks of the jinn and the demons, will descend to you. Moreover, they are in charge of the children of Adam's actions and protect them against all harm. If you summon any tyrannical King thereby who disobeys you, they will burn him. These are the names:**

Kaytāharāsh [كيتاهراش], **Ṣabā** [صبا], **Kayhīsh** [كيهيش], **Halīlī** [هليلي], **Wahash** [وهش], **Harhūsh** [هرهوش], **Hūrash** [هورش], **Sha'yāl** [شعيال], **Adamīsh** [ادميش], **Ba'nūj** [بعنوج], **Yā Rūkh** [يا روخ], **Yamīnākalhā** [يميناكلها], **Ṭāṭ** [طاط], **Kaṣahāt** [كصهات], **Shalāhamā** [شلاهما], **Ṭāhaṣ-haṣā** [طاهصهصا], **Haṣ-haṣā** [هصهصا], **Hajhajā** [هجهجا], **Hajhajā** [هجهجا], **Anūkh** [انوخ], **Anūkh** [انوخ]. **Majestic is God, blessed are His names, and exalted is His glory. None but Him is omnipotent, and none but Him is worthy of worship.**

Explanation: Glory be unto You, O Glorious One who is praised. Glory be unto You, O Ever Subsistent One who is honored. Glory be unto You, O Resurrecter. Glory be unto You, O Inheritor. Glory be unto You, O Omnipotent One. Glory be unto You, O knower of secrets. Glory be unto You, Who will resurrect all who are in the earth and the heavens. Glory be unto You, O subjugator of all creatures. Glory be unto You, Whom harm does not befall. Glory be unto You, O preordainer of sustenance. Glory be unto You, O creator of time. You are exalted in Your heaven, and Your status is elevated. You are highly exalted above what the oppressors say.

Know, my friend—may the Divine One guide you—that you can fulfill worldly needs by these majestic names. If you invoke God thereby and request a need, He will fulfill it. If you say them and request the presence of a spirit, he will come to you quicker than a flash of lightning. If you say them in a state of cleanliness from filth and in a clean place, the angel in charge of them

will appear to your right; ask him about whatever you wish and he will fulfill it for you. If you seek a spirit, you will take revenge on him. You can use the names, by the permission of the Lord Most High, in all conjurations, summonings and employments of the Ruhaniyyah of the planets (for the seven planets are under the earth's firmament). You can also use them for protection, healing, abduction, evil, reproval, and frightening. Among their servants, whom you can employ under the earth's firmament, are four angels who are in charge of the spirits: the angel Mahqā'īl [مهقائيل], the angel Ṭalahkafā'īl [طلهكفائيل], the angel Rūqā'īl [روقائيل], and the angel Ṣamṣamā'īl [صمصمائيل]. The seven archangels are in charge of the jinn and the devils under the earth's firmament. They are also the masters of flames, bewilderment, abduction and burning. Under each one of them are countless angels who you can employ in works both great and small.

I have completed the supreme Canopies and the grand Heavens to the last of the seven firmaments, to the earth, along with the employment of their Ruhaniyyah, their conjurations, and their instructions. However, there were no citations of incenses for you, but I shall now cite those incenses, by which independence will occur and by which you will evoke good fortune. They are frankincense, mastic, nadd (stick incense), and aloeswood. These four are for the uppermost Heavens and the seven Canopies. In addition to the four, costus and amber are for everything below them, to the earth's firmament. Then, after the incenses, I shall discuss the means by which aim is set aright and by which we will be safe from criticism, namely, communication from the angels, employable under the earth's firmament, who are in charge of the forelocks of the jinn and the devils—they are the twelve angels who sent down the twelve armies of jinn. Afterward, I shall discuss their seals, spears, appearances, names, conjurations and the secrets that characterize them. These were revealed through the tongue of Jibrā'īl [جبرائيل], the messenger to Adam (peace be upon him), then to Enoch (peace be upon him), who was of the wise, then from prophet to prophet and so on, down to the wise Solomon. These are the righteous supplications and purified names that are answered, by which the first and last of the spiritual angels, with their exalted ranks and lofty degrees, glorify.

His [the prophet Muhammad's] saying was, "Indeed, God has ninety-nine names. Whoever memorizes them will enter paradise. I shall first begin with the angel Mīṭaṭrūn [ميططرون], who is the last of the Kings and one of those in charge of, and empowered over, the jinn. We shall discuss the manner of employing him, his seal, his spear, his banner, his conjuration, his secret, his subjugation, and his uses, arranged according to topic.

Seal And Conjuration For The Angel Metatron

If you wish to employ this angel, fashion a ring from gold, with carnelian for its stone. Make and engrave it on a Friday when Venus is in its exaltation, which is Pisces; or on a Saturday, when Saturn is in Libra; or on a Sunday, when the Sun is in Aries; or on a Monday, when the Moon is in Taurus; or on a Thursday, when Jupiter is in Cancer and free from Gemini. Whatever time you choose to make it should be free from malefic aspects. Moreover, you should undertake this during the Arabic months that are not sacred. Thereafter, you neatly engrave it; wash it with running water and salt, then with rose water and musk and make a case for it from green silk. Then you prepare yourself, by the permission of the Divine, to conjure him.

This is the manner of Mīṭaṭrūn's [ميططرون] seal:

نطير عر كل يال

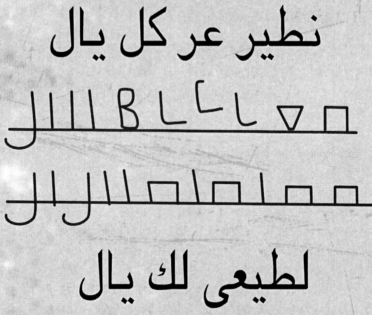

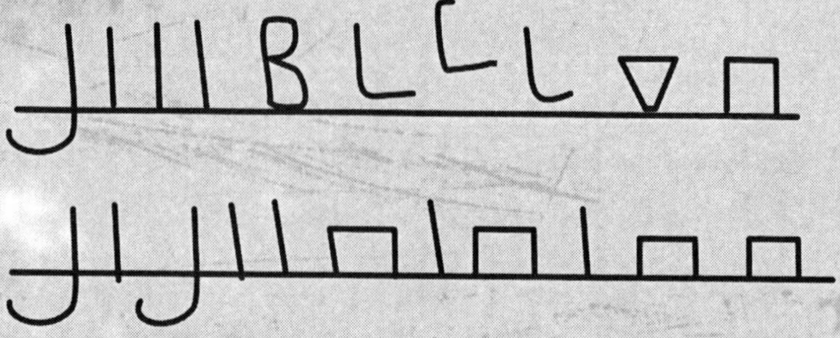

لطيعى لك يال

When you wish to inscribe it, betake yourself to a clean, pure, furnished house, fumigated with fragrant incense, and let the seal hang from a red or green silk thread. Then, prepare yourself for the Lord Most High, seeking that He subordinate the angels to you for whatever you wish. You shall abstain from eating anything having a soul, as well as what exists from it; let your food be of what the earth brings forth. Seclude yourself from others, except when it is indispensible.

Humble yourself before God Most High during your observation. Your vision and attention shall be with your heart. You shall sit facing the Holy Place. Avoid idle talk and keep to recitation and glorification. Sleep not unless it over-

comes you. Be careful not to eat food touched by a woman who is menstruating or having post-natal bleeding, and let neither one enter your home, as this will be better for your operation. Do not sit down, except in a state of purity.

Call down the spirit with words that subordinate him, at the beginning of the night; in the middle of the night; at the end of the night, before sunrise; at the beginning of the day, after the sun rises and becomes white; after the sun's zenith; and before the sun becomes yellow. Do not summon him after dawn, during the sun's zenith, or during sunset, as it will likewise be better for your operation. Fast frequently. On the fourth night, you will hear a rumbling like thunder in the sky. If you are in the wilderness, draw a circle around yourself, write the Burning Names in new saucers which neither food nor oil has touched, wash them off with water, and spinkle the circle for fear of the Divers from among the jinn. Likewise, let there be a shawl with amulets and Burning Names written on it on your head, lest the Flyers snatch you. Let your incense always burn during the conjurations.

Fear not, for one who possesses the seal has nothing to fear; rather, only one who fears destruction for oneself feels fear. Furthermore, avoid impurities at all times, as it is better for your work. After you complete seven days, angels of light will descend on you, and all the Ruhaniyyah of the earth will come to you. Thereupon show them the card, that is, the supreme seal of

Mīṭaṭrūn [ميططرون], for it is their pact, their subjugation, and a barrier between you and them. These are the names:

El, Shala' [شلع], Ya'ū [يعو], Yūbiyah [يوبيه], Beyah [بيه], Beyah [بيه], Betakfayah [بتكفيه], Betakfāl [بتكفال], Shaqāl [شقال], Qayā'īl [قيائيل], Mūraṣ [مورص], Marayūqad [مريوقد], Qadqāsh [قدقاش], Ṣamdarash [صمدرش], Ṣamdarash [صمدرش], Layth [ليث], 'Azī [عزي], Ṭārish [طارش], Darhash [درهش], Yahweh, Ah [اه], Ah [اه], Layṭa [ليطا], Ṭafyāsh [طفياش], Yūh [يوه], Ghash [غش], Ṣaṣmūs [صصموس], Jash. Do as ye are commanded!

You can also recite them with all conjurations. When the Kings, with their lofty ranks, exalted degrees, and diverse and frightening appearances, come to you, turn away from them and invoke God Most High to subordinate the angels, who are in charge of them and who have them by the forelocks, to you. When he descends to you, and the manifest light envelopes you, fortify your heart, strengthen your heart and yourself, and do not be afraid, for you have nothing of which to be afraid. Speak to him and he will speak to you. Do not let go of the seal, as long as he is with you. If he grants you obedience on your saying: "Obedience unto the Lord and His names, O Mīṭaṭrūn [ميططرون], you and your brothers. I entreat you to be my aide in whatsoever I seek assistance with regarding obedience to the Creator and what pleases Him," pray for him and then dismiss him, for the seal is finished

and your obedience is completed. After that, hold fast to purity, piety, fear of God Most High, mercy and compassion, good character, selflessness, charity, fasting, cleanliness, pleasant odor, and sympathy towards all creatures, and avoid the opposite, in everything you do. Seek all help from the Divine.

Supreme Conjuration For All Spirits

It is for all the spiritual angels, from the Throne to the Footstool:

In the name of Him by whose command the heavens stand, whom the angels glorify in different tongues, who created the heaven by His power, who spread the earth by His volition, who created the stars by His wisdom, who caused the seas to pour forth by His will, who dominates all things by His subdual and might, He of everlasting eternity before ancient times and past ages. Blessed is He in His luminous, elemental, eternal essentiality. He is hidden in the sanctity of the divine, exalted, everlasting lights, unperceivable to terrestrial humans, but established in pure minds. Blessed and holy are Your names, O Lord from whom the wisdom of spiritual spirits distinguished by exalted powers varies. Blessed and holy are Your names, and great is Your glory. None is omnipotent besides You. None is subduing besides You.

I invoke You by Your most beautiful names and Your most exalted and supreme words that You said to all things—Be!—whereupon that which You willed, happened, and which no earth or heaven can bear hearing. I ask You to subordinate to me Your slaves and angels that I might—though ultimately, I seek help from You—seek help from them for that which pleases You. I summon you, O company of pure spirits obedient unto El, Lord of the Worlds, from among the spiritual angels in charge of the forelocks of the jinn and the devils, by that by which El adjured the heavens and the earth, whereupon they obediently came by His power; by the supreme words and most exalted verses; by El, who is Lord of the hereafter and this world; by that which Jibrīl [جبريل] (peace be upon him) revealed to Solomon for all the prophets.

O Ehieh Asher Ehieh, Adonai Tzabaoth, El Shaddi, Nūr al-Nūr [نور النور], Ah [اه], Ah [اه], Tala'la' [تلألأ], by Hāh [هاه], Yāh [ياه], O Hū [هو], Hū [هو], Hū [هو], Shalīm [شليم], Namwāh [نمواه], Namwāh [نمواه], Ah [اه], Hayāh [هياه], Ṣahṣahā [صهصها], Haṣ-haṣā [هصهصا], Hajhajā [هجهجا], Ah [اه], Yah [يه], O Nūkh [نوخ], O Hiyah [هيه], Namūh [نموه], Namūh [نموه], by the name by which our Lord siezes all things, so that it

surrenders and becomes humble; and by the stored, hidden name: Ehieh Asher Ehieh, Ṣaṣfaṣ [صصفص], **Ṣaṣ** [صص], **Adonai Tzabaoth, El Shaddi. May God be pleased with you.**

Answer me, O angels of my Lord, O Shamakh Shaymīkhā [شمخ شيميخا], **by Him for fear of whom ye tremble, for great awe of Whom you fall down in a swoon, Who is clothed with awe, Who is hidden in glory, Who is crowned with light, the reflection of the radiance of Whose light shone upon Mount Sinai, whereupon it collapsed and flowed away, and the angels fell down from the air in a swoon, frightened by the sway of the Lord of the lofty Heavens, obedient unto His most beautiful names and supreme words; by the name that, if your soul were to say it, the heads of the cherubim angels would fall off: Hūrīn** [هورين], **Bārūkh** [باروخ], **Ashmakh** [اشمخ], **Shamākh** [شماخ], **the Exalted above all that is blessed, Ṭanṭīsh** [طنطيش], **Shafash** [شفش], **Akrākūk** [اكراكوك], **Ilāh** [إله], **Quddūs** [قدوس], **O He of might, O Hābūtarābakh** [هابوترابخ], **Bakh** [بخ]. **By ʻĀlim** [عالم], **Ṭaymūthā** [طيموثا], **Ṭaythā** [طيثا], **Manīʻā** [منيعا], **Shadāyid al-Arʻād** [شدايد الارعاد] **Ṭaythā** [طيثا], **Shamakh** [شمخ], **Qayyūmā** [قيوما], **Raḥmānā** [رحمانا], **Yūthā** [يوثا], **Māyūthā** [مايوثا], **Hūlāyin** [هولاين], **Halhīthā** [هلهيثا], **Qaẓ** [قظ], **Qaṭ** [قط], **Allah** [الله], **Allah** [الله], **al-Wāḥid** [الواحد], **al-Qahhār** [القهار], **Hū** [هو], **Hū** [هو], **Hūraṣ** [هورص], **Hūghān** [هوغان], **Kabbārā** [كبارا], **Jabbār** [جبار], **Abya'** [ابيض], **Bī'** [بيض], **Māyūt** [مايوت]**—majestic and mighty is the power of the names of Shatamūt** [شتموت]. **By Maṣūrash**

[مصورش], **Ṣaṣ** [صص], **Ṣamadī** [صمدي], **Hū** [هو], **Mīṣ** [ميص], **Tahmīṣ** [تهميص], **Ṣaṣ** [صص], **Hū** [هو], **Mayṣaṣayā** [ميصصيا], **Ṣaṣmūmah** [صصمومه], **Hūthāh** [هوثاه]. **O Fashṭalīs** [فشتليس], **Hū** [هو], **Maṣaṣayā** [مصصيا], **Hū** [هو], **King of the earth and the heavens**. **Answer me**, **O Mīṭaṭrūn** [ميططرون]. **Yah** [يه], **Yah** [يه],**Yah** [يه],**Yah** [يه],**Yah** [يه],**Yah** [يه],**Yah** [يه], **Beyah** [بيه], **Beyah** [بيه], Ū**rayāl** [اوريال], **Barkhayāl** [برخيال], **Hūrayāl** [هوريال], **Shūrayāl** [شوريال], **Raghshayāl** [رغشيال], **Hūrayāl** [هوريال], **Lahfāyāl** [لهفيال], **Barqayāl** [برقبال], **Nūrayāl** [نوريال], **'Ashayāl** [عشيال], **Ghashayāl** [غشيال], **Hadrayāl** [هدريال], **Lahfāyāl** [لهفيال], **Barqayāl** [برقبال], **Nūrayāl** [نوريال], **'Ashayāl** [عشيال], **Ghashayāl** [غشيال], **Qalāyāl** [قلايال], **'Adhrayāl** [عذريال], **Sarkhayāl** [سرخيال].

Blessed is our Lord—how powerful is His might!—**who restrained the jinn by His words**; **there is no god but Him**. **Hurry**, **by the** *kāf* [كاف] **in** *Kāf* [كاف], **the** *sād* [صاد] **in** *Ṣādiq* [صادق], **Ah** [اه], Ū**hī** [أوهي], **Shūṣah** [شوصة], **Sharmah** [شرمة], **Shaṭūr** [شطور], **Ḥā Mīm 'Ayn Sīn Qāf** [حمعسق], **Alif Lām Mīm** [الم], **Alif Lām Mīm Ṣād** [المص], **Rabb** [رب], **O most magnificent Majestic One** [جليل الأجل]. **Answer me**, **O Mīṭaṭrūn** [ميططرون], **You and all your aides**, **in obedience to El and His names**.

Second Conjuration For The Angel Metatron

I summon you, O company of pure spirits obedient unto El, Lord of the Worlds, by El, my Lord and your Lord, Creator of all things, God of all things. He is powerful over all things, wherever you may be in the kingdom of El, Mighty and Majestic. By the right of Mashṭāṭ [مشطاط], Ṭāṭ [طاط], Nūh [نوه], Nūh [نوه], Shawāh [شواه], Shawāh [شواه], Alhā [الها], Alhā [الها], Shamakh [شمخ], Ashnāl [اشنال], Ashnāl [اشنال], El [ال], El [ال], 'Ashyāl [عشيال], 'Ashāl [عشال], Marnayāsh [مرنياش], Ṣabūsh [صبوش], Yūsh [يوش], Marnayūsh [مرنيوش], Sayāsh [سياش], Mayūsh [ميوش], Yūsh [يوش], Marnayūsh [مرنيوش], Mayāsh [مياش], Yūsh [يوش], Ah [اه], Hawāh [هواه], Hū [هو], Hū [هو], Lord of Light Most High, hasten, O angels of my Lord. By the right of Shamwāsh [شمواش], Habūṭ [هبوط], Ah [اه], Ah [اه], Hawāh [هواه], Kaykanāsh [كيكناش], Marnayāsh [مرنياش], Mayūsh [ميوش], Nūsh [نوش], Nāsh [ناش], Līkhā [ليخا], Līkhā [ليخا], hurry unto me, O angels of my Lord; hurry unto me, O angels of my Lord."

Third Conjuration For The Angel Metatron

I summon you, O company of pure spirits, by the name of El, Lord of the heavens and the earth, knower of the unseen and the seen. He is the Merciful, the Compassionate, the King, the Holy, the Complete, the Source of Security, the All-vigilant, the Invincible, the Overpowering and the Glorious. Transcendent is He above that which they associate with Him. He is God, the Creator, the Maker and the Fashioner. His are the most beautiful names. All that is in the heavens and the earth glorify Him. He is the Invincible, the Wise. His command is mighty and His decree is inevitable. Everything will perish, while He is El, the Everlasting.

Yah [يه], **Yah** [يه], **Yāh** [ياه], **Yūh** [يوه], **Shamʿaṣayā** [شمعصيا], **Shamʿayā** [شمعيا], **Taqayāsh** [تقياش], **Taqīnash** [تقينش], **Hū** [هو], **Hī** [هي], **Badā** [بدا], **Bafarṣakīl** [بفرصكيل], **Yūkh** [يوخ], **Ashāmaṣaq** [اشامصق], **Ṣaṣ** [صص], **Ahnūsh** [اهنوش], **Shanāsh** [شناش], **Kafāk** [كفاك], **Shahāwah** [شهاوه], **Hū** [هو], **Hī** [هي], **Ashahā** [اشها], **Hū** [هو], **Hī** [هي], **Samā** [سما], **Ahyanūhayā** [اهينوهيا], **Balkhajīsh**

[بلخجيش], **Ṭahīsh** [طهيش], **Tamūsh** [طموش]. **Answer ye**, **by the names of the Divine**: **Alfaqayāhā** [الفقياها], **Shanqaṭūhā** [شنقطوها], **Wayā** [ويا], **Kaythā** [كيثا], **Nūr** [نور], **Yahaqān** [يهقان], **Nahayūh** [نهيوه]; **by Ehieh** [اهيا], **Ehieh** [اهيا], **Yā** [يا], **Nū** [نو], **Nū** [نو], **Hū** [هو], **Hū** [هو], **Kalnahāl** [كلنهال], **Allah**, **Allah**, **Nūth** [نوث], **Nūth** [نوث], **Kanthayūt** [كنثيوت], **Hū** [هو], **Hū** [هو], **Hū** [هو], **Yah** [يه], **Kayfahar** [كيفهر], **Kayfahar** [كيفهر], **Shabārish** [شبارش], **Bayākūnakh** [بياكونخ], **Ajīfūth** [اجيفوث], **Barāhayā** [براهيا], **Adnāwī** [ادناوي], **al-Raḥīm** [الرحيم], **Ḍabnatī** [ضبنتي], **Ṣayṣīm** [صيصيم], **Ẓayẓīm** [ظيظيم], **Jaythamūt** [جيثموت], **Mathbūn** [مثبون], **Sagh** [سغ], **Wayk** [ويك], **Saṭmaṭī'** [سطمطيع], **Ṣaṣ** [صص], **Ṣaṣ** [صص], **Ash** [اش], **Kūkh** [كوخ], **Ramakh** [رمخ]. **Barhayā** [برهيا] **will submit for fear of You**, **O Lord**.

Fourth Conjuration For The Angel Metatron

Say: **'Almahshāshiq** [علمهشاشق], **'Alamū** [علمو], **Thayākalamūthayā** [ثياكلموثيا], **Athyāligh** [اثيالغ], **Ṣa'ṣa'ā** [صعصعا], **Ṣa'ṣa'ā** [صعصعا], **Bahāṭā** [بهاطا], **Aṭālayā** [اطاليا], **Aqāliyā** [اقاليا], **'Asha'** [عشع], **'Ajaj** [عجج], **Sharmadī** [شرمدي]. **Blessed is El, the Magnificent**, **Ashaṭīkh** [اشطيخ], **Ṭayṭahā** [طيطها], **Ṣa'ṣa'ā** [صعصعا], **Jahāṭā** [جهاطا], **Aṭāliyā** [اطاليا], **Aqāliyā** [اقاليا], **'Asa'** [عسع], **'Ajaj** [عجج], **Sarmādi** [سرمادي]. **Blessed is El, the Magnificent**, **Ashaṭīkh** [اشطيخ], **Ṭayṭahā** [طيطها], **Malīkh** [مليخ], **'Alyākh** [علياخ], **Malīkh** [مليخ], **Shalmīth** [شلميث], **Qamwārish** [قموارش], **Halhanūsh** [هلهنوش]. **O Shamlahūsh** [شملهوش], **O Ṣa'ṭalaf** [صعطلف], **O Ṭalfīf** [طلفيف], **O 'Ayqafna'** [عيقفنع], **O Mashnaṣīr** [مشنصير] **Nūfayl** [نوفيل], **O Barīhūth** [بريهوث], **O Dayfūb** [ديفوب], **O Ṭanṭafīkh Aqahūsh** [طنطفيخ اقهوش], **O Shamlīkh Dalahūthā** [شمليخ دلهوثا], **O Shamkhīthā** [شمخيثا], **O 'Aṭlayākh** [عطلياخ], **O Shamlakh Qaṭīkh** [شملخ قطيخ], **O Shāhalhanīk Baqayūrash Ṭamqathīthā** [شاهلهنيك بقيورش طمقثيثا].

Answer me, O angels of my Lord. All that are in the heavens and on earth will swoon, except such as God pleases. All will come unto Him humbled. Shake Ṭaḥīṭamfīliyāl [طهيطمفيليال] **for them, O companies of Ruhaniyyah. Answer me, O Ṭaḥīṭamfīliyāl** [طهيطمفيليال]. **Stun him or else God will stun you. Hasten, O Ṭāṭamṭayāl** [طاطمطيال], **O Ṣa'ṭakyāl** [صعطكيال], **O Saṭnayā'īl** [سطنيائيل], **O Ghayfahfayā'īl** [غيفهفيائل]: **sieze ye him by the right of Jibrīl** [جبريل], **Mīkā'īl** [ميكائيل], **Isrāfīl** [إسرافيل], **and 'Azrā'īl** [عزرائيل]. **Hasten, O Ṭaḥīṭamfīliyāl** [طهيطمفيليال]. **Hasten, O Mīṭaṭrūn** [ميططرون].

Fifth Conjuration For The Angel Metatron

Say: Answer me, O Mīṭaṭrūn [ميططرون], **by Him who said unto the heavens and the earth, Come willingly or unwillingly, to which they replied, we will come willingly. Answer by God's names: O Ma'alqayūṣ** [معلقيوص], **O Manalqayūrash** [منلقيورش], **O Shamkhīthā** [شمخيثا], **O 'Almīthā** [علميثا], **O Ṭaymūthā** [طيموثا], **O Ṭaṭūrash**

[ططورش], **O Daymūthā** [ديموثا], **O Saqalqayūrash** [صقلقيورش], **O Ṭahaṭ-hayūkh** [طهطهيوخ], **O Rayhūn** [ريهون], **O Raqmayūsh** [رقميوش], **O Damhalūkh** [دمهلوخ], **O Ghaythūkh** [غيثوخ], **O Daymūkh** [ديموخ], **Adonai Tzabaoth**, **Alwahīmā** [الوهيما], **Mabūthā** [مبوثا], **Shaman** [شمن], **O ʻAlyāhīkh Darjah Bashāṭ** [علياهيخ درجه بشاط], **O Mūthā** [موثا], **O Thāf Ṣarīʻā Shārahwā** [ثاف صريعا شارهوا]. **Answer me**, **O Mīṭaṭrūn** [ميططرون], **wherever you may be in the kingdom of God**, **Mighty and Majestic**, **Tūlī** [تولى], **Awīl** [أويل], **Ḥath** [حث], **Baqṭāṭ** [بقطاط], **Laṭākhī** [لطاخي], **Aṭ** [اط], **Ḥathqash** [حثقش], **Lūliyah** [لوليه], **Lathqārīn** [لثقارين]. **Answer me**, **Wathrāyā** [وثرايا], **by the right these names have over you**.

Sixth Conjuration For The Angel Metatron

Say: **By Yūkhashāh** [يوخشاه], **Maghan** [مغن], **Māh** [ماه], **Maʻramāh** [معرماه], **O Adharīn Adharīn** [اذرين اذرين], **by Shanṭā** [شنطا], **Shanṭā** [شنطا], **Khadarūsh** [خدروش], **Dayūsh** [ديوش]. **Answer ye**, **by**

the right of Him who is crowned with light and power and glory, He is from whom you tremble in fear and fall down in swoon, out of awe. By Yā Lakūthā [يا لكوثا], **Fajhamīsh** [فجهميش], **Yūqash** [يوقش], **Bahīthā** [بهيثا], **Shalūthā** [شلوثا], **Yāqūtā** [ياقوتا], **Ṭaṭmā** [ططما], **Ṭaṭūfā** [ططوفا], **Shahīsh** [شهيش], **Mahrash** [مهرش], **Hū** [هو], **Hū** [هو], **Hū** [هو] **give your obedience unto God, O Mīṭaṭrūn** [ميططرون]. **Answer me, for Thrāyā** [ثرايا] **is a bright, flaming fire upon him who disobeys the names of God. Answer me, by Kalkathūm Hu Ṭiyah** [كلكثوم هو طيه].

Seventh Conjuration For The Angel Metatron

All Ruhaniyyah are obliged to obey this. Say: Answer me, O company of angels of the Lord of the Worlds, who were created from the light of the Divine. Wherever ye may be in the the kingdom of God, Mighty and Majestic, I conjure you to quickly answer and obey, by that which I have said unto you and am now saying; by El, El, Yāh [ياه], **Yāh** [ياه], **Hah** [هه], **Karagh** [كرغ], **Ramakh** [رمخ]. **May Barhayā** [برهيا] **submit**

for fear of You, O Lord, al-Aḥad [الأحد], **al-Aḥad** [الأحد], **al-Aḥad** [الأحد], **al-Fard** [فرد], **aṣ-Ṣamad** [الصمد], **Ṣamad** [صمد] **Kandarūd** [كندرود], **Knower of things before their existence, He who manifested Himself unto the mountain, crumbling it into a mound, whereupon Moses fell down in a swoon. Descend, O Mīṭaṭrūn** [ميططرون], **with heed, obedience, and compliance.**

Know, may the Divine guide you, that when you have completed seven days in the manner I have described to you, he will show himself to you, and his light will envelope you, and his subduing spirit will enclothe you.

Make a carpet for yourself from any kind of metal or fabric you wish, written on in black; on it you will sit, stand, and order the spirits as you are sitting. If that is not possible, use a piece of pure, clean parchment written on with a mixture of saffron, ink, musk, camphor and rose water. Thereupon you will achieve dominance over every soul on earth, human and jinn alike. You shall do likewise when employing terrestrial spirits concerning a seal or the like. God Most High willing, we will give the instructions, commentary, and names for the carpet in a separate chapter,

Sunday And Its Employable Ruhaniyyah

Say: **Answer**, **O angel Rūqayā'īl** [روقيائيل], **and you**, **O Ṭaqyā'īl** [طقيائيل], **by the right of these names**: **Yajarjayūn** [يجرجيون], **Elyon**, **Samāyūth** [سمايوث], **'Adnayūn** [عدنيون], **Samārūt** [سماروت], **Jabarūt** [جبروت], **'Adalūb** [عدلوب], **Kafalūb** [كفلوب], **Da'ūb** [دعوب], **Day'ūb** [ديعوب], **Shalūb** [شلوب], **Shaṭūb** [شطوب], **Ahīl** [اهيل], **Ahlīl** [اهليل], **Marmalayāl** [مرمليال], **Ḥarmalayāl** [حرمليال], **Kaqlīl** [كقليل], **Daykūb** [ديكوب], **Dayda'ūb** [ديدعوب], **Shayṭī'ā** [شيطيعا], **Shamṭī'ā** [سمطيعا], **Layṭa'ā** [ليطعا], **Yaṭa'** [يطع], **Sha'kanā** [شعكنا], **Shamhalayūb** [شمهليوب]. **Answer**, **O angel Rūqayā'īl** [روقيائيل], **by the right of these names**, **and you**, **O Ṭaqyā'īl** [طقيائيل], **by the right of these names**: **Yajarjayūn** [يجرجيون], **Elyon**, **Shamāyūn** [شمايون], **'Adnayūn** [عدنيون], **Shamārūt** [شماروت], **Jabarūt** [جبروت], **'Adalūb** [عدلوب], **Lahūb** [لهوب], **Shalahūb** [شلهوب], **Ẓamṭaḥā** [ظمطحا], **Mūth** [موث], **Lūb** [لوب], **Kafalūb** [كفلوب], **Da'ūb** [دعوب], **Day'ūb** [ديعوب], **Salūb** [سلوب], **Saṭūb** [سطوب], **Ahyal** [اهيل], **Ahyalīl** [اهيليل], **Ḥarmalayāl** [حرمليال], **Kaqlīl** [كقليل], **Daykūb**

[ديكوب], **Dayda'ūb** [ديدعوب], **Sayṭa'ā** [سيطعا], **Samṭa'ā** [سمطعا], **Layṭa'ā** [ليطعا], **Yaṭa'** [يطع], **Sha'kanā** [شعكنا], **Shamhalayūb** [شمهليوب]. **Answer, O angel Rūqayā'īl** [روقيائيل], **by the right of these names**: **Aqareamī** [اقرتمي], **Bashṭawākhash** [بشطواخش], **Fī** [في], **Fāq** [فاق], **Yā** [يا], **Khal** [خل], **Alḥarā** [الحرا], **Baḥjarīshā** [بحجريشا], **Ṭūshīshā** [طوشيشا], **Ṭawā** [طوا], **Adfī'** [ادفيض], **Aẓhar** [اظهر], **Harī** [هري], **Aykah** [ايكه], **Aykah** [ايكه], **Shamī** [شمي], **Kaydah** [كيده], **Arah** [اره], **Dharah** [ذره], **Kay-ānā** [كيانا], **Wūmā** [ووما], **'Abdah** [عبده], **Saya'lamah** [سيعلمه], **Dādūmah** [دادومه], **Kab** [كب], **Kamah** [كمه], **Adākamah** [اداكمه], **Ay** [اي], **Yamarūh** [يمروه], **Bakh**, **Bakh**, **Bakh**, **Bakh**, **Bakh**, **Ṭā** [ط], **Ṭā** [ط], **Hah** [هه], **Hah** [هه], **Hah** [هه], **Hah** [هه], **Ah** [اه], **Ah** [اه], **Ah** [اه], **Ah** [اه], **Hih**, **Hih**. **Hurry to me, O angels of my Lord. Answer me, O Rūqayā'īl** [روقيائيل], **and you, O Ṭaqyā'īl** [طقيائيل].

Seal Of The Angel Of The Sun

Inscribe it when the Sun is in its exaltation, during the first hour of the first Sunday of the month, and set it out under the stars at

the beginning of the month. This is the seal, just as you see it:

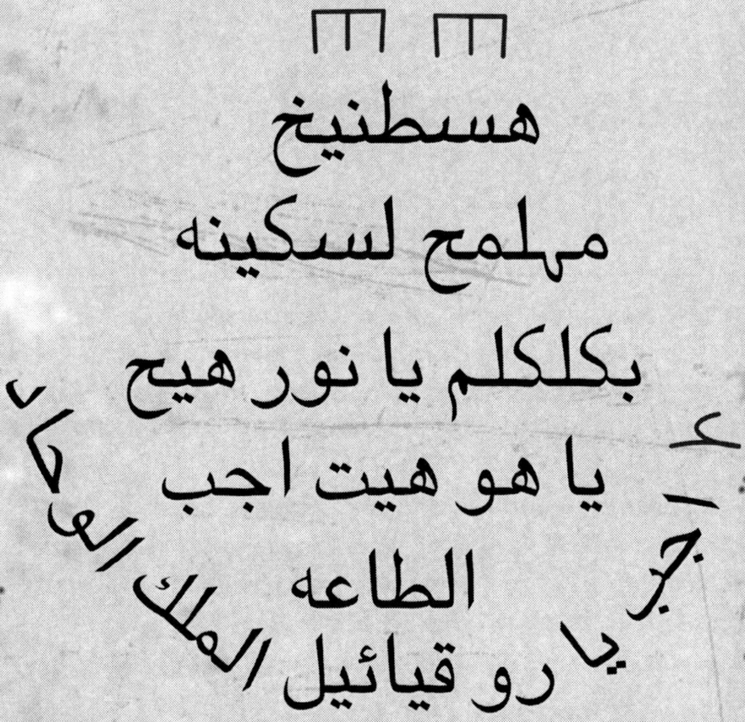

Inscribe these names on the setting of the gem.

The Companies Under The Sun Who Can Be Employed

They are fiery and are possessors of lightning. The conjuration compels them to be subservient, obedient, and compliant. Say:

I summon you, O company of pure spirits obedient unto God, Lord of the Worlds, by the names with which God created you, which are written upon the Sun; by Shahshah [شهشه], **Hayl** [هيل], **Ṭashak** [طشك], **Ṭasha'īl** [طشعيل], **Būh** [بوه], **O Ṣaymawī** [صيموي], **O Way'ūd** [ويعود], **Bahaylayūh** [بهيليوه], **al-Arkayāẓ** [الاركياظ]; **by Haybūh** [هيبوه], **Haybūh** [هيبوه], **Nūr** [نور], **Nūr** [نور], **Hayshabūh** [هيشبوه], **Kashrayāwub** [كشرياوب], **Shalahūb** [شلهوب], **Ya'anshaqūm** [يعنشقزم]; **by 'Alshaqūm** [علشقوم], **'Alshaqūm** [علشقوم], **'Alshaqūm** [علشقوم], **Shūṣal** [شوصل], **Haybarash** [هيبرش], **Yada'ūb** [يدعوب]. **Blessed is the Light of Light, the Director of Affairs, the Destroyer of Tyrants, Haykh** [هيخ]. **Answer me, O company of fiery ones, by the right of that with which the angels of the Sun glorify.**

The Names Of The Sun

With the permission of God Most High, you can employ them for burning. They are as follows: By Hashalyasa‘ [هشليسع], **Ṭab‘alaḥ** [طبعلح], **Kalkalam** [كلكلم], **Ṭalīṭ** [طليط], **Aṭlaṭ** [اطلط], **Ya‘mak** [يعمك], **Ḥatyak** [حتيك], **Aklak** [اكلك], **Hashlash** [هشلش], **Shalmaṭī‘** [شلمطيع], **Ṭī‘** [طيع], **Ya‘ṭaf** [يعطف], **Laqaṭ** [لقط], **a fire that Hārish** [هارش] **inhabits. Answer me, O Hārish** [هارش], **by the right that Shaghūb** [شغوب] **has over you; burn and shock.**

Write them in a cup, wash them off with water, and sprinkle the possessed person's face with it and the possessing jinni will burn. They are for reproval, subjugation, conjuration, and burning any rebel jinni or devil.

Concerning The Terrestrial Jinn King Of The Sun

He is al-Madhhab [المذهب], a king of great stature, potent obedience, and speedy compliance, who is crowned. He is of Banu Dahir ibn 'Uwaymir ibn Sharhabil al-Jan Jamlith. For aides, he has rebel jinn, and Ruhaniyyah in numbers only the Lord, Mighty and Majestic, can enumerate. Following is the noble seal. Inscribe these names on the setting of the gem and set it out under the stars with the seal. They are as follows:

الاهم ١١ا ٢١ الواحد القهار ١١١ بح الرد الوحاه امساعلا

Monday And Its Employable Ruhaniyyah

Of Ruhaniyyah, it has a number of angels that none but the Lord Most High can enumerate, and presiding over them is the king al-Abyadh [الأبيض] (**Marrah** [مرة]).

Seal Of The Angel Of The Moon

أجب ياجبريل

شطط كططش

طبسط سلس طسه

نوهيًا هو مياط هو

حاده اجل وعزالله

هو هوا ساكلا

الملك

Conjuration To The Companies Of Aquatics Between The Heavens And The Earth Of Whom Qamrayael [قمريائيل] Is In Charge

You say: **Mahū** [مهو], **Tanshīr** [تنشير], **Maynāsh** [ميناش], **Wadareīsh** [ودرتيش], **Yashīn** [ياشين], **Abat** [ابت], **Aytā** [ايتا], **Qanshūr** [قنشور], **Ashkhalīkh** [اشخليخ], **Aydalakh** [ايدلخ], **Waṭarṭūrīkh** [وطرطوريخ], **Bayshārūd** [بيشارود], **Hajakh** [هجخ], **Hū** [هو], **Rashmīkh** [رشميخ], **Alhārabah** [الهاربه], **Bamshā** [بمشا], **Sharīd** [شريد], **Aqayẓayūnā** [اقيظيونا], **Ba'āwut** [بعاوت], **Mūt** [موت], **Adonai**, **Shūṭal** [شوطل], **Shaymīthāhim** [شيميثاهم], **Maghthānā** [مغثانا], **Shaklahūm** [شكلهوم], **Ṣanā** [صنا], **Sa'at** [صعت], **Ṭalayūnā** [طليونا], **Shahūh** [شهوه], **Fayfūnā** [فيفونا], **Lord of all things**, **Who watches over every soul and knows that which it earns**, **and Whose command all things obey**.

Conjuration To The Terrestrial King Al-Abyadh [الأبيض]

Say: I conjure you, O company of pure spirits obedient to El, Lord of the Worlds, from among the abductors, the sages, the seers, the soothsayers, the messengers, the flyers, the dwellers of the air and those who eavesdrop on the heavens. I conjure those of you who are throughout the earth, its lands and seas, of any of the heroic hosts, be ye far or near, weak or strong, obedient or obstinate, by that which Fayqaṭūsh [فيقطوش] **uttered, whereupon ye dismounted the air, falling, and got off the clouds, frightened, and your state of affairs went awry, and your sight was covered as you fled in a blind stupor, for their walls encompassed you and their clouds overshadowed you. By Hazmah** [هزمة], **Hazmah** [هزمة], **Mareamāth** [مرتماث], **Mareamāth** [مرتماث], **Qardamāt** [قردمات], **Qardamāt** [قردمات], **Basham** [بشم], **Ashlām** [اشلام], **Aqash** [اقش], **Arqash** [ارقش], **Fashaṭ** [فشط], **Fashalīṭ** [فشليط], **Jalhah** [جلهة], **Ḥajaj** [حجج], **Ḥajaj** [حجج], **Maṣrahūn** [مصرهون], **Kayd** [كيد], **Rawāyah** [رواية], **Maḥarīt**, **Hanad** [هند], **Barkhūf** [برخوف], **Hūf** [هوف], **Ḥawl** [حول], **O Ḥawl** [حول], **Aṭaṭ** [اطط], **Aṭaṭ**

[اطط], **Anūkh** [انوخ], **Anūkh** [انوخ], **Alkhūsh** [الخوش], **Alkhūsh** [الخوش], **Mayhūshash** [ميهوشش], **Hūsh** [هوش], **Hūt** [هوت], **Yāhūt** [ياهوت], **and by the right these names has over you, to quickly answer and obey**: **Ghāshayā** [غاشيا], **Māshayā** [ماشيا], **Qadūyāl** [قدويال], **Awāh** [اواه], **Awāh** [اواه], **Karab** [كرب], **Karab** [كرب], **Saṭūh** [سطوح], **Shafāh** [شفاه], **Jarhatah** [جرهته], **Jarhatah** [جرهته]. **He who answers not the caller of El will neither escape in the earth nor have protectors besides Him—such are in manifest error**. **Answer me, O Abya'** [أبيض], **you and your aides, by the right these names have over you**: **Hayhah** [هيهة], **Haylā** [هيلا], **Hayhūt** [هيهوت], **Hayā** [هيا], **Hayān** [هيان]. **In whatsoever part of the earth ye may be, hasten, hasten, hasten, hasten**.

Instructions For Al-Abyadh's Seal

On the setting of the gem, inscribe the following: There is no god but El. All things shall perish, save His countenance. His is the judgment and to Him ye will be returned.

Following is the seal, just as you see it:

| ا كا ١٢ر ٦/ا ٤ع ١ٍ٦٨ كا ١٨ كه |
| ككه ١٥ اط ١١١ ط ١٩ ١١١ ط ١١١ ط |
| ككه ١ه اط ١١ الل ١ل ٧ ٦٩ ككه |
| لكه ١١١ طارال ٩ ١ط ١١ ط ٥ه |

اياه لشطخ يا هور عاه
أجب بالطا عه يا أبيض

الطاعه لله يا أبيض

| ١١١١ ٦١ ط ٧ ح |
| كه ١ر ه ١ كه ككه |

قل اللهم مالك الملك

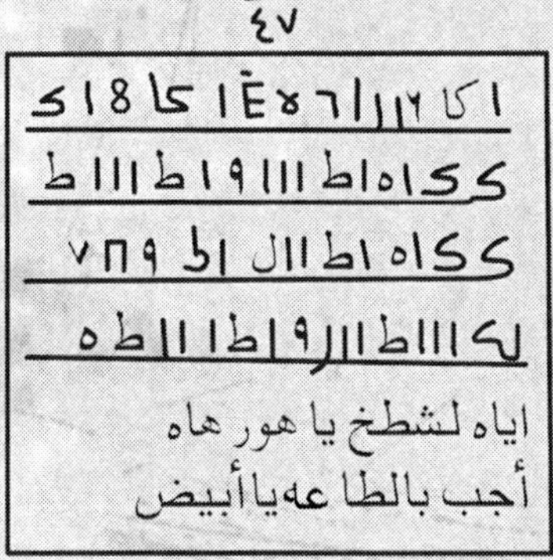

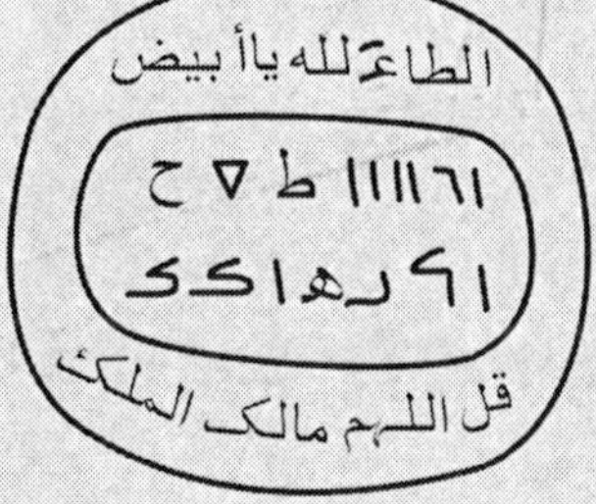

THE NAMES OF AL-ABYAḌH'S AIDES

Answer me, **O Abu al-Ḥakam** [أبو الحكم], **and you, O Hishām** [هشام], **and you, O Hawhar** [هوهر], **and you, O Shaḥanīt** [شحنيت], **O Maṣ-faraṣ** [مصفرص]. O righteous slaves of El, wherever ye may be, El will bring you all together. Surely He is able to do all things.

Tuesday and Its Employable Ruhaniyyah

Know, may the Lord guide you, that Mars, the swordsman of celestial bodies and of great obedience, governs this day. It has a number of angels that none but God Most High can enumerate, and Samsamā'īl [سمسمائيل] **is in charge of them and oversees them. The conjuration is to him and all the angels who glorify on the planet Mars (peace be upon them). Say:**

I conjure you, O Samsamā'īl [سمسمائيل], **and you, O Damyā'īl** [دميائيل], **and you, O Jalhayā'īl** [جلهيائيل], **and you, O Shardayā'īl** [شرديائيل], **and you, O Raqṭayā'īl** [رقطيائيل], **by the right of that with which the angels glorify on the planet Mars; by the name with which El will raise the dead to the place of standing on the Ḍay of Judgment; by Jaydūsh** [جيدوش], **Jaydūsh** [جيدوش], **Kalkalaytūsh** [كلكليتوش], **Alyashmaṭūsh** [اليشمطوش], **Abrahaj** [ابرهج], **Ḥalhatkahā** [حلهتكها], **Jaljayūh** [جلجيوه], **Rabb** [رب], **Ṭūb** [طوب], **Almaḥaḥyā** [المححيا], **'Awj** [عوج], **Rabb** [رب], **Aḥad** [أحد], **Hī** [هي], **Hī** [هي], **Daryūkh** [دريوخ], **Adonai Tzabaoth, El Shaddi. Hasten, Hasten, O inhabitants of Mars.**

The Sword Of Mars

Fashion a sword from Indian iron and inscribe it with the following names when Mars is in its exaltation, which is Capricorn. Then set it out under the stars for seven days and nights, just as you did with the seals, and it will perform all the functions of the seals. These are the names you inscribe thereon: Karayūsh [كريوش], **'Adārayūsh** [عداريوش], **by 'Ayūsh** [عيوش], **'Ānash** [عانش], **Barshānah** [برشانه], **Yazīdūsh** [يزيدوش], **Ka'akh** [كعخ], **Baydashīs** [بيدشيس], **Kadwā** [كدوا]. **O dwellers of the most exalted star**! **O Mars**!

The Conjuration Of Mars

By Qamhar [قمهر], **Qamhar** [قمهر], **Qarqar** [قرقر], **Jarayūsh** [جريوش], **Sharhayūsh** [شرهيوش], **El**, **Khūsh** [خوش], **Hū** [هو], **Hū** [هو], **the Lord of Light Most High**.

The Seal of Samsamael [سمسمائيل]

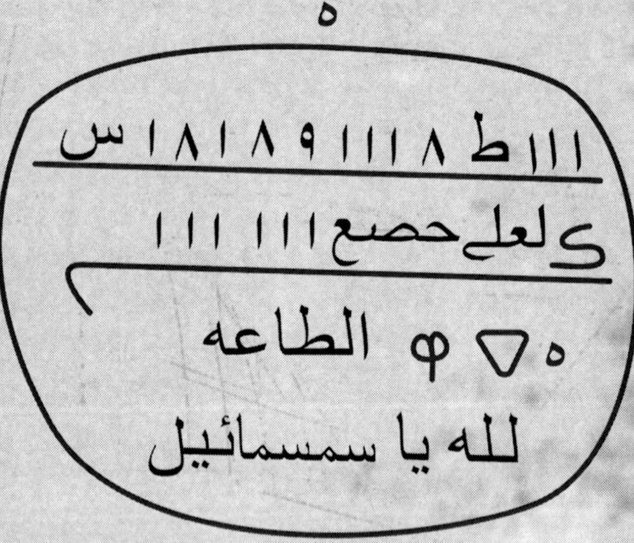

Inscribe these symbols on the sword along with the names: **How perfect is my Lord**, **Wadarhūsh** [ودرهوش], **Munṣif** [منصف], **Naslakhāt** [نسلخات], **Balsāt** [بلسات], **Yaṭlīkh** [يطليخ], **Aw** [او], **Lakh**

[لخ], **Lakh** [لخ], **Lakhakh** [لخخ], **Kaḥmalakh** [كحملخ], **Aw** [او], **Yanjar** [ينجر], **Baqṭalayūn** [بقطليون], **Rahwāb** [رهواب], **Bah** [به]. **They were overturned therein**: **they**, **the misguided**, **and all the hosts of Iblis**.

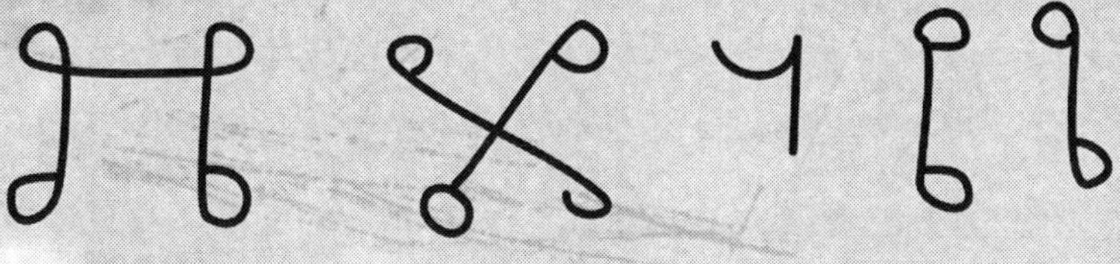

It also has a spell for rending unconscious those who are possessed, **and forcing their possessing spirits to manifest**. **It is as follows**: **Ha'malas** [هعملس], **Ṭamas** [طمس], **Jalayūs** [جليوس], **Hayalūs** [هيلوس], **Falayūs** [فليوس], **Hayṭalūs** [هيطلوس], **Samalūn** [سملون], **Awahūs** [اوهوس], **'Alayūs** [عليوس], **Balsaṭān** [بلسطان]. **Hasten**, **by the right of the One**, **the Triumphant**. **Make him to manifest**, **O Aḥmar** [أحمر].

Instructions For The Killing Of An Evil Jinn By Al-Ahmar [الأحمر]

If a possessing jinni or Wind rebels against you, and you wish to kill him or expel him from a body, then draw a picture of him and the angel in charge of the spirits of the jinn upon a clean parchment or a clean floor. Write these names upon his neck so that they extend across his shoulders:

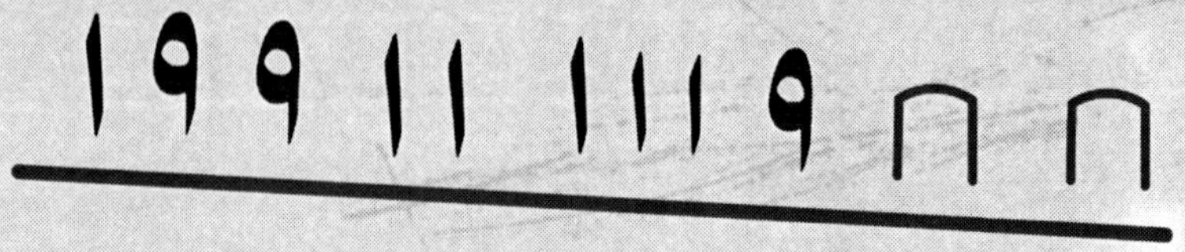

On his right arm and right side, you write:

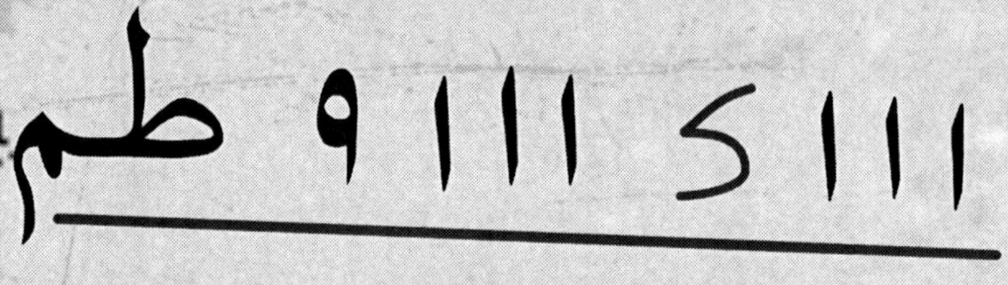

On his left arm and left side, [you write]:

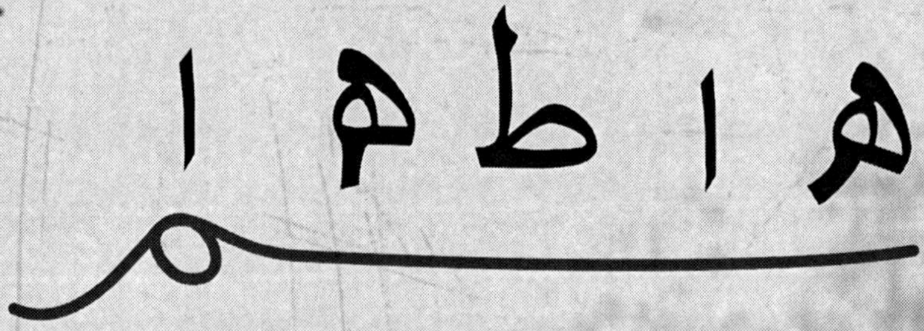

On his right leg and right shin, write 'Ḥajaj [حجج]' on his left leg and left shin, 'Encompass them'; and on his belly, these pure, sacred names, which are feared by all the spirits, that is, the angels and the jinn, and which constitute a binding pact upon them, and which is the Greatest Name:

When you wish to seek vengence against the Wind, draw this image and strike it with a rope attached to a pomegranate branch and he will awaken and adjure you by the Lord Most High not to kill him. If he requests a pact, agree to it and make a pact with him; then write an amulet for him and let him go. If he returns, and he is Muslim, punish him and imprison him, and if he is a disbeliever, kill him. But hasten not to kill, for therein is harm and evidence of one's rancor, none of which befit the kindess of sages. If he declines to speak, rebels, trangresses, and refuses to come out, write the names that are in the image. Summon the angel in charge of them, Mīṭaṭrūn [ميططرون]; summon the Ruhaniyyah of the seven planets. Say three times, "This is indeed an enemy who has rebelled, trangressed, and disobeyed El Most High," and insert the spear into any of the letters you wish and he will die. Alternatively, if you cut it with scissors, bit by bit, as you evoke, he will be cut into pieces, just like the paper. Therefore, guard, my brother, what has reached you, namely, this image, which is an independent treatment, and which can be employed in three hundred types of real magic pertaining to treatment and the like. Use it only for that of which the Lord Most High approves and your reward will be in this life and the next.

If someone brings a person afflicted by a Wind to you, write the names on his body, just as you wrote them on the image, and summon the Ruhaniyyah of the planets. Carry a knife with you and, for whatever part of the body the person informs you of, insert the knife into the first letter of that line so that the Wind can exit his entire body. Do likewise for anyone afflicted by a Wind, regardless of which part of the body he is in.

If you have someone suffering from conjunctivitis brought to you, stab the first name in the image with a knife, and continue stabbing, letter after letter, until he leaves him. Do likewise for pain in any part of the body.

Know, my brother, that this is a secret of secrets. Therefore, guard it and do not disclose it to an ignoramous, for he will employ it in that which is neither permissible for him nor pleasing to God Most High. Impart wisdom only to those deserving of it, for they are worthier of using it.

Wednesday And Its Employable Ruhaniyyah

It is for King Burqān [برقان] and the angel in charge of him, Mīkā'īl [ميكائيل], the intimate of God, who has the Ruhaniyyah by the forelocks, and who stands on the left hand of power.

The Conjuration Of The Angel Of Wednesday

You say: Answer me, O Mīkā'īl [ميكائيل], by the right of the names written upon your forehead: 'Shahān [شهان], Shawīn [شوين], Kafānūsh [كفانوش], Lūnīm [لونيم], Kaylīm [كيليم], Ya'ṭīsh [يعطيش].' O God, O Qadīm [قديم], O Ḥayy [حي], O Muḥyī [محيي], O Dā'im [دائم], O Bāri' [بارئ], O Fard [فرد], O Wāhid [واحد], O Ṣamad [صمد], answer my supplication and subordinate to me Your servant Mīkā'īl [ميكائيل]—surely You are able to do all things. How excellent a protector! How excellent a helper!

Conjuration Of The Ruhaniyyah Of Thunder

Their chief is Dardayā'īl [دردیائیل]. **You say**: **Adyah** [ادیه], **Sha'āwūn** [شعاوون], **Mas** [مس], **O Darmāy** [درماي], **Shawkal** [شوكل], **Shaymamā** [شيمما], **Mīm** [ميم], **Yashmūmā** [يشموما], **Mīm** [ميم], **Haytā** [هيتا], **Ṣaṣaq** [صصق], **Maqtānā** [مقتانا], **Shalalhamūm** [شللهموم], **Waynawā** [وينوا]. **Answer me**, **O company of Ruhaniyyah**!

Instructions For The Ruhaniyyah Of Wednesday's Seal

With the blessing and aid of the Lord Most High, **fashion it from white silver and a green stone**. **Inscribe thereon the names written on the forehead of Mīkā'īl** [ميكائيل]. **There-**

after, set it out under the stars in the prescribed manner to complete your operation. Of Terrestrials, it has the supreme king Burqān [برقان]—he of majestic appearance and quick compliance. Of Ruhaniyyah, it has a number that only God Most High can enumerate.

If you wish to make use of him, then fashion a ring from pure silver for him and set it out under the stars according to the number of planets. Then inscribe thereon seven planets, each in its day and hour. When the inscription is completed, wash it with running water and salt and set it with a green stone. The first thing you inscribe thereon shall be the image of a crab in whose mouth is a locust. You encircle that with seven planets, that is, the glyphs of the seven planets. After that, you prepare yourself for his conjuration and manifestation, so that he may appear for you. You shall prepare in seclusion from others, in a clean, pure house furnished with all manner of furniture. The seal you shall hang between three rose bay branches, but if none of those is available, then between three boxthorn branches; it shall hang between them by a green silk thread. You shall call him down at the beginning of the night, the end of it, and the middle of it, twenty-one times each time. Do likewise during the daytime. On the fourth night, when everyone is asleep, and after having evoked him, you shall go to a crossroad and dig a cubit-deep hole in clean earth there, drop the seal therein, evoke him seventy-one times, and cover the hole. Then, after having slaughtered an animal for him as an act of hospitality and taken its blood, you shall return home. With this blood, you shall then write the seal on a pentacle of marble or a clean parchment, hang it at the place of the seal, and evoke him as usual. On the sixth night, you will hear a roar or cry from it, but fear not. (It will persist in this manner.)

On the seventh night, he will show himself to you and speak to you and bring the seal to you (he will speak to you in a language you understand). The sign of his arrival will be his opening the door and then closing it, and your feeling calm. He will adjure you by the mighty pacts and request things from you that are difficult for you; answer him not, for he is testing you and taking notice. He will then say to you, "You must entertain me to the best of your ability." Then he will remain with you and continue to be at your disposal in three hundred types of needed illusions and real magic, great and small. If you wish something to be brought to you—whether it is in the east, the west, a vault, or a person's house—he will inform you of it and bring it to you. He will cling to you and not leave you. Say the names, "Answer, O Kashīrah [كشيره]," or say, "Answer, O Burqān [برقان]," while the seal is in your pocket. You should be clean of body and clothes, and persistent with the work and with cleanliness. Beware of malodorous sweat and breath, a contemptuous state, and intermingling with ostentatious persons. The servants will serve and befriend him, and he will bring them vast quantities of money.

Ma'adaryus said: "I asked the Perfect Nature about the status of this seal, its repute, its marvels, its uses, and the speed of its response (only the Lord Most High can enumerate the number of servants and aides it has.) Thereupon all of its hosts and troops became manifest to me. He then told me wondrous stories and strange things. It brings near whatever it wills and distances whatever it wills. If it brings near, it is by the permission of the Divine, Glorious and Exalted, and by the power of His names. None but you alone can sever it."

Say: "O Burqān [برقان], do such and such." The sage Ma'adaryus said, "The Perfect Nature likewise told me that it informed him about the art of magic and jihad, and that it used to transport him over a distance of a month's journey in a single hour."

Instructions for Burqan's Seal

Inscribe the names below the stone along with the covenant. They are as you see:

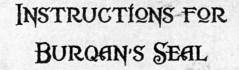

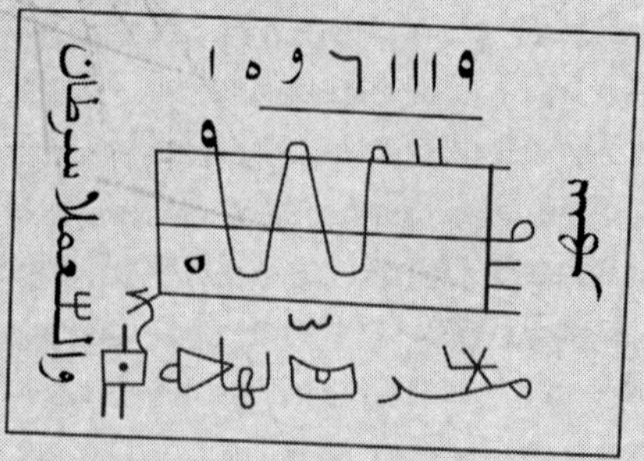

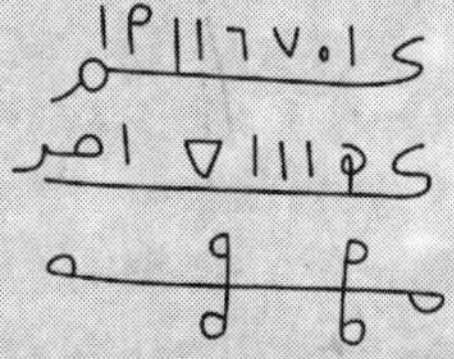

The First Conjuration To The King Burqan [برقان]

Say: **In the name of El, my Lord and your Lord, the Creator of all things, who has power over all things. 'Surely your Lord is God, who created the heavens and the earth in six days and is firmly established on the Throne, directing all things. There is no intercessor except after His permission. That is the Divine, so worship Him. Will you not receive admonition?'** (**Quran** 10:3) (**Repeat** 265 **times) Blessed is El, Lord of the Worlds. I summon you, O company of pure spirits created of the fire of hot wind, from among the abductors, the sages, the seers, the soothsayers, the flyers, the divers, the dwellers of the sky, those who eavesdrop on the heavens,**

and all the heroic armies from among the Stalker Jinn, the Cyclones, the Danāhishah [دناهشة], the Qafāshah [قفاشة], the Nashāṭishah [نشاطشة], the Killers, the residents of Sind and India, the inhabitants of the clouds, those who take shelter in the fog, those who roam the air, and those of you who are of Banū Kaylakh [بنو كيلخ], Banū Sa'lī'ah [بنو سعليعه], Banū Ghurāb [بنو غراب], Banū Hawān [بنو هوان], Banū Khawbah [خوبه], Banū 'Awjah [بنو عوجه], Banū Karfajah [بنو كرفجه], Banū Nabaldī [بنو نبلدى], Banū Alsatā [بنو الستا], Banū Yakūsh [بنو يكوش], Banū 'Āṣim [بنو عاصم], or Banū al-Afqam [بنو الأفقم], by the conjurations of al-Dāfūn [الدافون]—the jinni who resides upon mountain peaks—which Faytaṭūsh [فيتطوش] uttered, whereupon ye dismounted the air, falling, obedient and compliant, and ye got down from the clouds, terrified, and your state went awry and your sight was covered as you fled in a blind stupor, for their canopies surrounded you, their clouds overshadowed you, and their flames shot at you; and by Hazamāt [هزمات], Hazamāt [هزمات], Mareamāt [مرتمات], Mareamāt [مرتمات], Afardamāh [افردما], Anūkh [أنوخ], Anūkh [أنوخ], Ankaftiyah [انكفتيه], Ankaftiyah [انكفتيه]. Haste, O Burqān [برقان], by the right of these names with which the Divine One created you: 'Hīt [هيت], Hīt [هيت], Ḥat [حت], Ḥat [حت], Aywāt [ايوات], Ṭat [طت], Ṭat [طت], Ṭatiyah [طتيه], Shayrakh [شيرخ], Shayrakh [شيرخ], Bakhat [بخت], Bakhat [بخت], Kaṭ [كط], Kaṭ [كط], Ṭat [طت], Mashrahīt [مشرهيت], Sharhayūt [شرهيوت], Sarhayūt [سرهيوت], Ayāwut [اياوت], Aykūt [ايكوت], Aykūt [ايكوت], Maytā [ميتا],

Maytā [ميتا], **Sharārikh** [شرارخ], **Sharārikh** [شرارخ].' **By the right of Jarī** [جري], **I adjure you to answer**. **O Barākh** [براخ], **Barākh** [براخ], **Kabarāsh** [كبراش], **Kabarāsh** [كبراش], **Mahārish** [مهارش], **Mahārish** [مهارش], **Fāqūqiyah** [فاقوقيه], **Fāqūqiyah** [فاقوقيه], **Hāraqīqah** [هارقيقه], **Shayzahamz** [شيزهمز]. **Hasten**, **hasten**, **hasten**, **O Burqān** [برقان]!

The Second Conjuration To The King Burqan [برقان]

Say: **By Rasūs** [رسوس], **Sharāwash** [شراوش], **Mahar** [مهر], **Mahar** [مهر], **Hārish** [هارش], **Hārish** [هارش], **Sham** [شم], **Barsham** [برشم], **Karsham** [كرشم], **Karsham** [كرشم], **Mashkan** [مشكن], **Mashkan** [مشكن], **Qaryah** [قرية], **Qaryah** [قرية], **Handah** [هندة], **Handah** [هندة], **Barhah** [برهة], **Hābarah** [هابرة], **Manwah** [منوة], **Manwah** [منوة], **Barah** [برة], **Māhūt** [ماهوت], **Mashwah** [مشوه], **Majrah** [مجره]. **Hasten**, **obediently**, **O Burqān** [برقان]. **By the the right of the name with which I summoned you**, **I adjure you to make haste**, **heedfully**, **obediently**, **quickly**.

The Third Conjuration To The King Burqan [برقان]

Say: **'Aj** [عج], **'Aj** [عج], **Ja'** [جع], **Akhūq** [اخوق], **Ajrawā** [اجروا], **A'mawā** [اعموا], **A'mū** [أعمو], **Aqwā** [اقوا], **Barqā** [برقا], **Ḥamā** [حما], **Ṭayqā** [طيقا], **Dayūsh** [ديوش], **Dayūsh** [ديوش], **Yalash** [يلش], **Quddūs** [قدوس], **Qabūsh** [قبوش], **Shūrīsh** [شوريش], **'Arwāwāsh** [عرواوش], **Quddūs** [قدوس], **Quddūs** [قدوس]. **'Give thanks, O household of David—very few of my servants give thanks.' Hasten, O Burqān** [برقان]. **Thereupon you will hear blowing and whistling from them until he appears for you**.

The Fourth Conjuration To The King Burqan [برقان]

Say: **Fūq** [فوق], **Fūq** [فوق], **Barqūq** [برقوق], **Barqūq** [برقوق], **Fūq** [فوق]. **By that which is in Qab** [قب], **Qab** [قب], **Barq** [برق], **Yarṣa'ā** [يرصعا], **Yarṭīqā** [يرطيقا], **Artaqūqā** [ارطقوقا], '**Arsūsī** [عرسوسي], **Aḥramūh** [احرموه], **Māzūqā** [مازوقا], **Fūq** [فوق], **Barqūq** [برقوق]. **O Marqab Qab Maraq** [مرقب قب مرق], **O Burqān** [برقان], **hasten**!

The Fifth Conjuration To The King Burqan [برقان]

Say these words while burying the ring: **Hīt** [هيت], **Hīt** [هيت], **Kayṭab** [كيطب], **Kayṭab** [كيطب], **Hab** [هب], **Hab** [هب], **Hū** [هو], **Hū** [هو], **Kaf** [كف], **Kaf** [كف], **Barīkh** [بريغ], **Barīkh** [بريغ], **Datar** [دتر], **Datar** [دتر], **Adyā** [اديا], **Waqsha'īr** [وقشعير], **Amat** [امت], **Amat** [امت]—**these are what I entrust unto you**, **O Burqān** [برقان].

The Sixth Conjuration To The King Burqan [برقان]

You say: **By Rafaqshakam** [رفقشكم], **Kaslasākh** [كسلساخ], **Taghmārish** [تغمارش], **Fayārish** [فيارش], **Farqash** [فرقش], **Nīs** [نيس], **Kashkam** [كشكم], **Kalsākh** [كلساخ]. **Answer by the glorification of the Cherubim and the praise of the Ruhaniyyah**, **O Burqān** [برقان] **the Heedless**, **wheresoever you are in the heavens and earth of the kingdom of the Creator**, **Mighty and Majestic**.

The Seventh Conjuration To The King Burqan [برقان]

Say: **Yūh** [يوه]; **Yūh** [يوه]; **Hayhalayūh** [هيهليوه]; **Hayhalayūh** [هيهليوه]; **Arkamayāṭ** [اركمياط]. **By Hayhūn** [هيهون], **Haybūr** [هيبور], **Kashrayāwub** [كشرياوب], **'Alshaqūm** [علشقوم], **Ayūrashā** [ايورشا],

Mayūr [ميور], **Ayūr** [ايور]. **'Light upon light**, **the Lord guides to His light whomsoever He pleases.' Hat** [هت], **Khat** [خت], **Hat** [هت], **Sharat** [شرت], **Ṭat** [طت], **Ayūlat** [ايولت], **Maythā** [ميثا]. **Appear**, **Watazāyā** [وتزايا], **by the right of the Exalted Name**. **O Burqan** [برقان]!

Thursday And Its Employable Ruhaniyyah

Of the brilliant planets, **Thursday has Jupiter and**, **of the spiritual angels**, **the angel Ṣarfayā'īl** [صرفيائبل]. **The conjuration is to Ṣarfayā'īl** [صرفيائبل] **and all the inhabitants of the sixth firmament**. **Say**:

I conjure you, **O company of obedient angels of the Divine who glorify Him**, **Lord of the Worlds**, **to answer**. **O angel Ṣarfayā'īl** [صرفيائبل], **by the right of that with which the angels in the sixth firmament glorify**, **and by the praise of the Spiritual Ones and the glorification of the Cherubim**: **Quddūs** [قدوس], **Quddūs** [قدوس], **Quddūs** [قدوس], **Qarūqas** [قروقس], **Mahyaṣ** [مهيص], **'Aymas** [عيمس], **Barqayās** [برقياس], **Yadahūrash** [يدهورش], **'Ayhūsh**

[عيهوش], **Manāmarqash** [منامرقش], **Haha'rash** [ههعرش]. **Blessed is the Lord of power and force. Glory be unto You, O Living One who does not die.**

Glory be unto You, Who is exalted above all things. Glory be unto You, Who will resurrect all the dead. Glory be unto You, Who is great in power and glory. Glory be unto You, Who subdues His servants by death and annihilation. You are blessed and exalted high above that which the oppressors say.

Instructions For Thursday's Angel's Seal

The seal of the angel Ṣarfayā'īl [صرفيائيل]: **With the aid of God Most High, fashion a ring of pure gold set with a ruby stone for it. This is its inscription: Haṭakh** [هطغ], **Ghāmiṣ** [غامص], **Ṣamad** [صمد], **Kandar** [كندر], **Yūd** [يود], **Knower of all things before their existence.**

Shamhurash Jupiter's Terrestrial King

The conjuration for Shamhūrash [شمهورش]: Fashion a brass ring for him on Thursday, in the hour of Jupiter, when it is in its exaltation, which is Cancer. Then wash it with water and salt and set it out under the stars in the normal manner. This is the seal of Shamhūrash [شمهورش]:

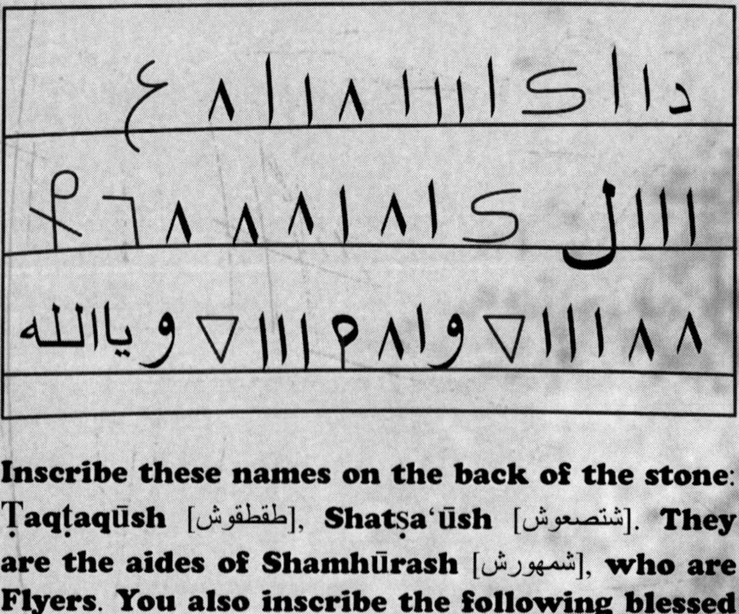

Inscribe these names on the back of the stone: Ṭaqṭaqūsh [طقطقوش], Shatṣa'ūsh [شتصعوش]. They are the aides of Shamhūrash [شمهورش], who are Flyers. You also inscribe the following blessed

names: Adonai Tzabaoth, El Shaddi. Answer you, by the leave of God.

Conjuration To The Company Of Flyers

You say: Yalmūtanas [يلموتنس]; **Saʻaydam** [سعيدم]; **Aḥyas** [احيس]; **Asrālaham** [اسرالهم]; **O Qaṭash** [قطش]; **Karaream** [كررتم]; **Anūkh** [انوخ]; **Anūkh** [انوخ]; **O Rūkh** [روخ]; **Naḥūmā** [نحوما]; **Hūhiyah** [هوهيه]; **Yadaʻūb** [يدعوب]; **Mahrāʻīl** [مهرائيل]; **O Marsaṭīf** [مرسطيف]; **O Marmarīl** [مرمريل]; **O Qarīl** [قريل]; **O Nahīl** [نهيل]. **Hasten, Hasten, O company of Ruhaniyyah, by the right of these names and that which they hold, and by Him unto whom all things yield, Who has power over all things.**

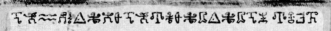

The Conjuration To Shamhurash And All The Flyers

After the first conjuration (that is at the beginning of the conjuration of Burqān) [برقان], **say**: **By Khalkhalīsh** [خلخليش], **'Aajalīn** [عجلين], **Ṭafsal** [طفسل], **Jaljamīsh** [جلجلميش], **Awyāq** [اوياق], **Awyāq** [اوياق], **Shamhūrash** [شمهورش], **Awyāq** [اوياق], **Yah** [يه], **Yah** [يه], **Yah** [يه], **Yāh** [يه], **Yāh** [يه], **Yīh** [ييه], **Yīh** [ييه], **Ahyā'īl** [اهيائيل], **Ehieh**, **Adonai Tzabaoth**, **Shamhūrash** [شمهورش], **Shamhūrash** [شمهورش], **Shamūhamrash** [شموهمرش], **Shamhayāl** [شمهيال], **Ra'yā'īl** [رعيائيل], **Ṣabūtā** [صبوتا], **Ṣīwānīl** [صيوانيل], **Damū** [دمو], **Raqūsh** [رقوش], **Admū** [ادمو], **Mayāl** [ميال], **Mayāl** [ميال], **Damhūmaṣ** [دمهومص], **Hūrash** [هورش], **O Mūṣ** [موص], **Shatramīs** [شطرميس], **Ṭarmas** [طرمس], **Fanjahūrash** [فنجهورش], **Kayd** [كيد], **Tahaylatyā** [تهيلتيا], **Darash** [درش], **Hanūsh** [هنوش], **Haytūqash** [هيتوقش], **Maṣaymūsh** [مصيموش], **Tūrash** [تورش], **Falīs** [فليس], **Nāsh** [ناش], **Qūsh** [قوش]. **Hurry and come unto me**, **Dahnash** [دهنش]! **Come unto me**, **Hūrash** [هورش]! **Come unto me**, **Sarayūsh** [سريوش]!

Qaymaṭarīsh [قيمطريش] **shall come. Shajārīsh** [شجاريش] **shall come. Hayṭībārish** [هيطيبارش] **shall come. Khandash** [خندش] **shall come. Shamhūrash** [شمهورش] **shall come. Hasten, Ṣanūsh** [صنوش], **Ṣanī** [صني], **Ardhī** [ارضى], **Ṣayṣīsharash** [صيصيشرش]. **Hasten, hasten, heedfully and obediently, by the leave of the Lord of the Worlds.**

Second Conjuration To Shamhurash

Y ou say: By Ṭaqyārish [طقيارش], **Shalhayūhash** [شلهيوهش], **Aljūsh** [الجوش], **Ṣayjūrab** [صيجورب], **Hayārish** [هيارش], **Sharaysanūnah** [شريسنونه], **Ḥarmash** [حرمش], **Fayqūmash** [فيقومش]. **Haste, O Shamhūrash** [شمهورش], **by the light of God's countenance, by which the heavens, the earth, and all that is therein exist. That is the Lord, besides Whom there is no god, the Almighty, the All-wise.**

Third Conjuration To Shamhurash

Say: By ʻAshʻāsh [عشعاش], Ṭaghyāsh [طغياش], Ṭarṭāsh [طرطاش], Ashnāh [اشناه], Astashrāh [استشراه], Wāh [واه]. Hurry, O Abū al-Walīd Shamhūrash [أبو الوليد شمهورش]. Come, O Ṭaqṭaqūsh [طقطقوش]. Come, O Salkhayā [سلخيا]. Come, O Maymūn [ميمون]. Come, O Shamardal [شرمدل]. Come ye, answer, listen, and obey, by O Ehieh; Adnamūh [ادنموه]; Kamash [كمش]; Shalḥam [شلحم]; Yakdash [يكدش]; and Mashkūrash [مشكورش], ʻbefore we efface faces and turn them hindwards, or curse them as we cursed the sabath-breakers. And the command of the Divine shall be executed.ʼ

Fourth Conjuration To Shamhurash

Say: ʻAṭaṭyūsh [عططيوش], Shafʻayūsh [شفعيوش], ʻAṭlayabūsh [عطليبوش], Kamshaqlayūsh [كمشقليوش], Ṭaylayūsh [طيليوش], Ahlasayūsh [اهلسيوش], ʻAṭaṭyūsh [عططيوش], Laṭaṭyāsh [لططياش], Ṭaylayūsh [طيليوش], Shaqlayūsh [شقليوش], ʻAlshahūsh [علشهوش], Qashlahūsh [قشلهوش], Maynayāsh [مينياش], Ṭaqṭayāsh [طقطياش]. Answer, O Shamhūrash [شمهورش]. Answer, O Ṭaqṭaqūsh [طقطقوش]. Hurry,

hurry, **Andabūsh** [اندبوش], **Aṣfaqār** [اصفقار], **Taltīsh** [تلتيش]. **Answer**, **O Abū al-Walīd Shamhūrash** [شمهورش], **by Ṭaylash** [طيلش], **Hal** [هل], **Yaṭūb** [يطوب], **Hamla'** [هملع], **Hā** [ها], **Shaṭūr** [شطور], **'Alyaṭūf** [عليطوف], **Hāf** [هاف], **Maṭū'** [مطوع], **Kashjara'** [كشجرع], **Kal** [كل], **Yaṭūqanī** [يطوقني], **Shaylaqūf** [شيلقوف], **Sharāyakab** [شرايكب], **Mashyalūb** [مشيلوب], **alone**, **without partner**. **Glory be unto Him**. **All things yield unto Him**.

Friday And Anael

Of the brilliant planets, **Friday has Venus and**, **of the Ruhaniyyah**, **the angel 'Anyā'īl** [عنيائيل]. **The conjuration to 'Anyā'īl** [عنيائيل]: **Answer me**, **O angel 'Anyā'īl** [عنيائيل], **and you**, **O angel Sam'ayayā'īl** [سمعييائيل], **and you**, **O angel Sharḥayā'īl** [شرحيائيل], **by the right of that with which the angels in the planet Venus glorify**; **by the names with which the Lord created you**; **by Ṭash** [طاش], **Ṭashūsh** [طشوش], **Ṭāsh** [طاش], **Ṭashī** [طشي], **Ahyā** [اهيا], **Ahyāsh** [اهياش], **Hamā** [هما], **Hamā** [هما], **Shāh** [شاه], **Hayshūsh** [هيشوش], **Ṣaymaṣa'** [صيمصع];

by Hā [ها], **Hashūsh** [هشوش]; **by Sharah** [شره], **Hayā** [هيا], **Hayā** [هيا], **Mara'** [مرض], **Māhā** [ماها], **Sharah** [شره]; **by Jarah** [جره], **Hayhūsh** [هيهوش], **Yaqshūsh** [يقشوش]. **Exalted is the Creator**, **al-Wāḥid** [الواحد], **al-Qahhār** [القهار], **al-Aḥad** [الأحد], **al-Fard** [الفرد], **al-Ṣamad** [الصمد], **al-Malik** [الملك], **al-Quddūs** [القدوس], **al-Mu'min** [المؤمن], **al-Muhaymin** [المهيمن], **al-'Azīz** [ال عزيز], **al-Jabbār** [الجبار], **al-Mutakabbir** [المتكبر]. **Unto Him belong praise and blessing. There is no god but Him, the Living and Ever Subsistent. Answer me, O angel 'Anyā'īl** [عنيائيل], **by the right of these noble names: 'Ḥajaj** [حجج], **Maṣrahūn** [مصرهون], **Ṭahshīrah** [طهشيرة], **Haydaj** [هيدج], **Maykalāj** [ميكلاج].**' Answer me, O angel 'Anyā'īl** [عنيائيل].

Conjuration To The Earthy Terrestrials

Say: Thakatā [ثكتا], **Thakatā** [ثكتا], **Awmahā** [اومها], **Thakatā** [ثكتا]. **And by the right of the Divine, by the strength of His might, by His glory, by His majesty, and by the power of His sovereignty. Make haste, O Zawba'ah Abāṭil Shamāyil Kafalūsh** [زوبعة اباطل شمايل كفلوش]. **'Verily**

those who oppose God and His messenger will be of those most humiliated.' Jahrash [جهرش], Ṭash [طش], Hashūr [هشور], O Saḥ [سح], Dha'ūn [ذعون], Shaṭūn [شطون], Ba'līl [بعليل], Fayūgh [فيوغ], Marakrayā'īl [مركريائيل], Shaflīf [شفليف], Shalaftahā [شلفتها]. Answer the invocant, O Zawba'ah [زوبعة], by Jahūr [جهور] and Lāhūr [لاهور]. He shall come by Yāh [ياه], Yāh [ياه].

Instructions For Zawba'ah's Seal And What Is Inscribed Thereon

With the aid of God Most High, fashion a ring from pure white silver on Friday, when its planet is in its exaltation; then inscribe it. After inscribing it, elevate it, wash it with rose water, cense it with aloeswood and nadd, place it in a green silk bag, and prepare yourself for the conjuration. Set it out under the stars in the prescribed manner, by the will of the Lord Most High, from whom you seek aid. Inscribe these names on the setting of the stone: Saldayāh [سلدياه] is humble by the name

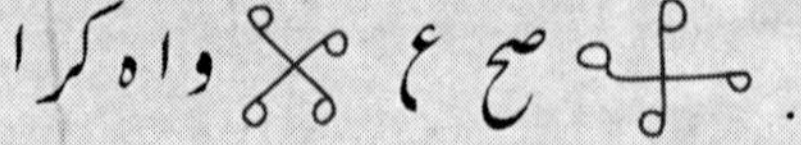

Saturday for Kasfayael

Its angel is Kasfayā'īl [كسفيائيل]. He is a celestial angel and his planet is the seventh. Seek help from him with all celestial bodies. Saturday has, of the spiritual angels, a number that only God Most High can enumerate. You can employ them in all works of piety.

Instructions for Kasfayael's Seal

Fashion a ring from jet or from agate that has been colored black, and write thereon in gold or silver. Set it out under the stars in the prescribed manner. This shall be in the hour of Saturn, on Saturday—the first hour—in the first week of the Arabic month, when Sat-

urn is in its exaltation, **if that is possible**, **otherwise when Libra is on the ascendant**. **These are the names that you write in the circle of the ring**: **Jarhashal** [جرهشل], **Rahāl** [رهال], **Bāṭalā** [باطلا], **Sakṭahūyaḥ** [سكطهويح], **Barahūyaḥ** [برهويح], **Ehieh**, **Ehieh**,**Naṭarkīwān** [نطركيوان], **Kīwān** [كيوان].

In the third circle, **you write these**: **Saṭalīḥ** [سطليح], **Halhalīḥ** [هلهليح], **Masādīḥ** [مساديح], **Malsayā** [ملسيا], **'Aṭlayhā** [عطليها], **Malhayā** [ملهيا], **Shafī'ā** [شفيعا], **Taṭū'a** [تطوعا]. **O company of tribes**! **Make haste**, **angel Kasfayā'īl** [كسفيائيل]!

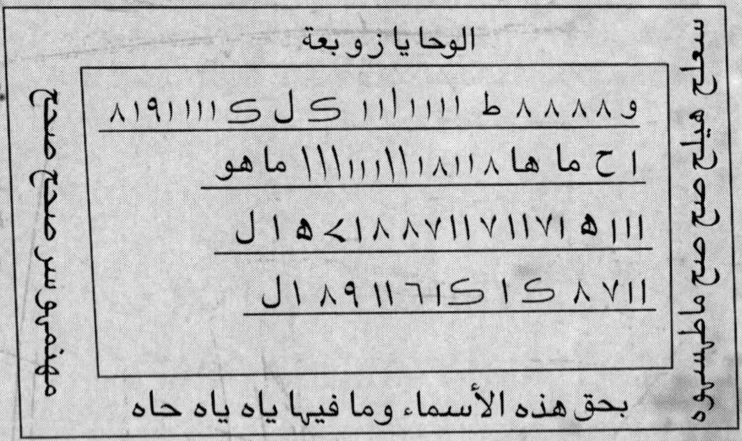
الوحا يا زو بعة
بحق هذه الأسماء وما فيها ياه ياه حاه

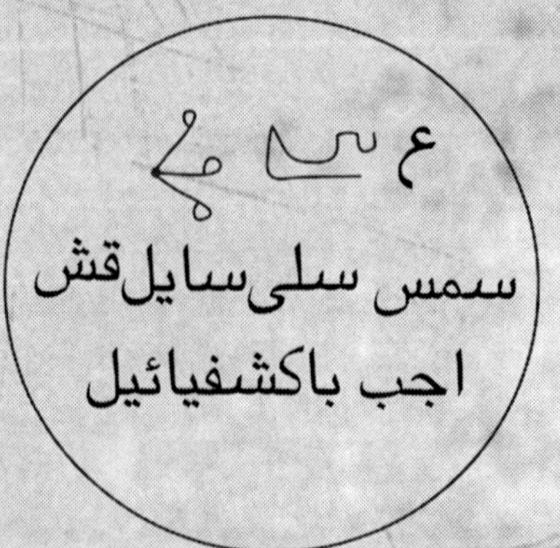
سمس سلى سايل قش
اجب باكشفيائيل

The Conjurations Of The Hidden Regions

These are the Conjurations of the Hidden Regions, as extracted from the Book of Regions, through which we become superior to all of humankind. They are for revealing cures, reproving spirits, and subjugating any of the Ruhaniyyah. Utter them only on important occasions. Say:

Answer me, O angel Kasfayā'īl [كسفيائيل], **by 'Araf** [عرف], **'Arfayāh** [عرفياه], **Ṭāh** [طاه], **Ṭāh** [طاه], **Ah** [اه], **Ah** [اه], **Yahwā** [يهوا], **'Arfayā** [عرفياه], **'Ahdayā** [عهديا], **Sham'adayā** [شمعديا], **Malakhīt** [ملخيت], **Ḥakamīn** [حكمين], **Hayd** [هيد], **Hayd** [هيد], **Āk** [آك], **Halam** [هلم], **'Aryā** [عريا], **Shamaydab** [شميدب], **Layūt** [ليوت], **Ṭasūm** [طسوم], **Ṭāsūm** [طاسوم], **Āyūm** [آيوم], **Ḥayūm** [حيوم], **Qāyūm** [قايوم], **Kamīrāwut** [كميراوت]. **Hurry, by the right of these names, and by the right of Him Who is exalted above the seven highest Heavens, Lord of the seven firmaments and the nethermost earths, who giveth death unto the living and life unto the dead. Haste ye, by Nafajtajā** [نفجتجا], **Najāj** [نجاج], **Najīj** [نجيج], **Ṭamūh** [طموح],

Bayrūkh [بيروخ], **Namḥayā** [نمحيا], **Maṣāqīm** [مصاقيم], **Mayālīkh** [ميااليخ], **'Azyāh** [عزياه], **Ah** [اه], **Wāh** [واه], **Mastaṭqāh** [مستطقاه]—**quickly**!—**Arṭāyīl** [ارطاييل], **Namūh** [نموه], **Namūh** [نموه], **Sharhayā** [شرهيا], **Sharmadāh** [شرمداه], **Darmakīl** [درمكيل]. **By the right of the Lofty Edifice, the First Word, and the Greatest Name, I entreat you to come, O company of terrestrial Ruhaniyyah in charge of the regions, heedful and obedient unto the names of the Creator, Lord of the Worlds. Hurry, hurry, hurry, hurry, by the leave of Him who says unto a thing, 'Be!' whereupon it is. 'Every obstinate tyrant will be brought, and each soul will come, and therewith will be a driver and a witness.'**

Of the Terrestrials, it has Abū Nūkh [أبو نوخ] **and, of the Aides and Rebels, a number only the Divine, Mighty and Majestic, can enumerate. Employ them in all things; they comply quickly.**

The Conjuration Employment And Seal Of Maymun

Fashion a ring from steel on Saturday, when Libra is on the ascendant. During that hour, inscribe it and wash it with running water and salt. Thereafter, make a bag

for it from white silk. Then set it out under the stars in the prescribed manner. After setting it out under the stars, elevate it upon your person.

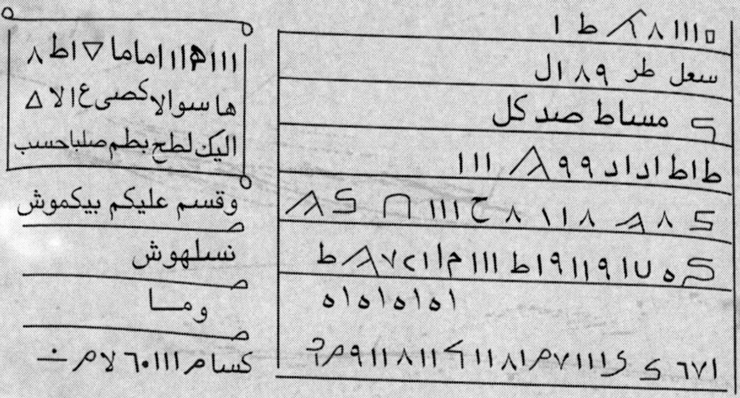

Conjuration To Maymun Aba Nukh And All The Flying Mayamonites

Speak this internally. Say: Malshāqish [ملشاقش], **Mahrāqish** [مهراقش], **Aqshāqish** [اقشاقش], **Saqamū** [سقمو], **Aqash** [اقش], **Aqash** [اقش], **Marqash** [مرقش], **Raqshā** [رقشا], **Rafīsh** [رفيش], **Rafshār** [رفشار], **Qasaṣīḥ** [قسصيح], **Naqamūsh** [نقموش], **Ghashafū** [غشفو], **Ṭamash** [طمش]. **I conjure you, Ghaykamūsh**

[غیکموش], **Danhalīsh** [دنهلیش], **Saqamū** [سقمو], **Nahash** [نهش], **Santaharash** [سنتهرش], **Amās** [اماس], **Ṭasūs** [طسوس], **Samqal** [سمقل], **Ṭahīl** [طهیل], **Qūsh** [قوش], **Ṭaghmārish** [طغماش], **Rahū** [رهو], **Amshū** [امشو], **Aṭashū** [اطشو], **Aṭash** [اطش], **Aṭash** [اطش], **Kashā** [کشا], **Markashīkh** [مرکشیخ], **'Alsāqish** [علساقش], **'Aqsīr** [عقسیر], **Maqsharāl** [مقشرال], **Khūsh** [خوش], **Hū** [هو], **Hū** [هو], **Highest Lord of the Light**, **Anūkh** [انوخ], **Adonai Tzabaoth**, **El Shaddi**, **Amraham** [أمرهم]. **Answer me, O Maymūn Abū Nūkh** [میمون أبو نوخ], you and your aides, by the right these names hold over ye.

WHAT IS SAID AFTER THE INTERNAL CHANT

ⲥⲟⲇⲑⲓⲝ⳥ⲉⲝⳑ⳹ⲥⲇⲟⲟⲧⳑⲉⲝⲝ⳼ⲉⲝⲩⲟⲟ ⲟⲁⲅⲅ⳥

Say: By **Ṭaqash** [طقش], **Taqash** [طقش], **Thalāmīn** [ثلامین], **Thalāmīn** [ثلامین], **Hayā** [هیا], **Hayān** [هیان] — in whatsoever part of the earth ye may be. By **Rahdah** [رهدة], **Rahdah** [رهدة], **Faqdah** [فقدة], **Faqdah** [فقدة], **Shaqah** [شقة], **Shaqah** [شقة], **Fūh** [فوه], **Fūh** [فوه], **Fūh** [فوه], **Hat** [هت], **Hat** [هت], **Qūt** [قوت], **Ṣāliḥ** [صالح], **Maṭaytakh** [مطیتخ], **Haṭayṭ** [هطبط], **Marqatīn** [مرقتین], **Danash** [دنش], **Nātiyah** [ناتیه], **Mantamūn** [منتمون], **Mal-**

jam [ملجم], **Maljadīn** [ملجدين], **Man** [من], **Sanmā** [سنما], **Salayṭa** [سليطا], **Almaṭāhalaykalā** [المطاهليكلا], **Maylūn** [ميلون]. **Respond by yourself**, **O Maymūn** [ميمون], **by Shamlīkh** [شمليخ], **Malmalīkh** [ململيخ], **Mādīkh** [ماديخ], **Malīsā** [مليسا], **'Aẓīmā** [عظيما], **Malmayā** [ملميا], **Shafī'ā** [شفيعا], **Taṭū'ā** [تطوعا]. **Answer**, **O company of tribes**, **by Namūh** [نموه], **Namūh** [نموه], **Hayd** [هيد], **Ahmā** [اهما], **Akwan** [اكون], **'Alūjah** [علوجة], **Jūl** [جول], **Jūl** [جول], **Ḥūl** [هول], **Jaḥqah** [جحقه], **Khaykhamah** [خيخمه], **Shahīmūthā** [شهيموثا], **Shabah** [شبه], **Wān** [وان], **Anyah** [انيه]. **'It sailed with them amid waves like mountains**. **And Noah called out to his son** (**who was standing aloof**), **"O my son**, **embark with us**, **and be not with the disbelievers**."' **By Ṭashāqish** [طشاقش], **Mahrāqish** [مهراقش], **'Aqash** [عقش], **Ma'shar** [معشر], **El**, **Khūsh** [خوش], **Hū** [هو], **Hū** [هو], **the Highest Lord of Light**, **Hāj** [هاج], **Law'ākh** [لوضاخ], **Anūkh** [انوخ], **Anūkh** [انوخ], **Malkahīkh** [ملكهيخ], **Quddūs** [قدوس], **Quddūs** [قدوس], **Ma'zal** [معزل], **Ḥafshan** [حفشن], **Yaqrayṭan** [يقريطن], **Jūl** [جول], **Jūl** [جول], **Faqash** [فقش]. **Answer by the honor of the Lord**, **by yourself**, **O Maymūn** [ميمون].

Al-Ahmar's Seal

Inscribe it on carnelian or gold on Tuesday, when Mars is on the ascendant. The seal is as you see:

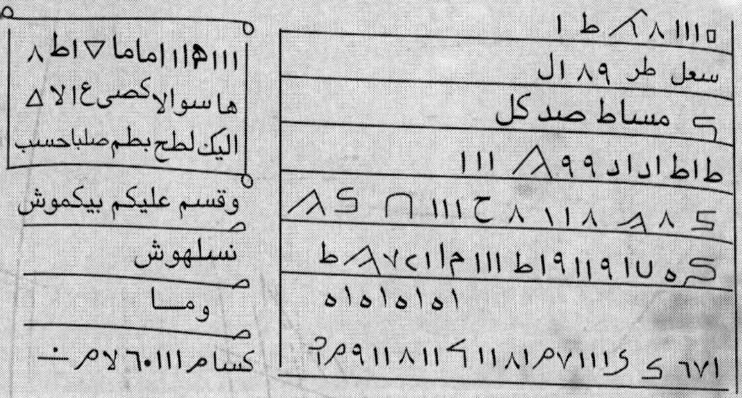

Say: Arṭāyil [أرطايل], **Marlafāyil** [مرلفايل], **Azahīl** [ازهيل], **Barahīl** [برهيل], **'Aṭafīl** [عطفيل], **Yaṭafīl** [يطفيل], **El, El, Haqīl** [هقيل]**—by the right of these names, I conjure you to answer. Set it out under the stars in the prescribed manner, which we have discussed.**

Conjuration Of The Fiery Lands

This is a conjuration capable of burning any spirit. Utter it only on important occasions. If one of the kings of the jinn, whether celestial or terrestrial, defies you, and you recite it, angels of light will descend to you, holding spears of light that burst in flames at whoever disobeys the Lord Most High. You say the following names:

By Ṭalṭālish [طلطاليش], **Ṭalṭālish** [طلطاليش], **Kalalash** [كللش], **Falqasha'ah** [فلقشعة], **Albaṭāyālīqā** [البطاياليقا], **Shanan** [شنن], **'Afaf** [عفف], **al-Ḥāfiẓ** [الحافظ], **El. You will perish suddenly, O enemy of El. Burn him, O friends of El, by Hajramīsh** [هجرميش], **Hajramīsh** [هجرميش], **Mīd** [ميد], **Ahūmā** [اهوما], **Alūn** [الون], **'Alūjah** [علوجه], **Halalmafū'** [هللمفوع], **Kamsalmakū'** [كمسلمكوع], **'Ashaljaj** [عشلجج], **Shalṭahūlaj** [شلطهولج], **Yadahūlaj** [يدهولج], **Shakalūj** [شكلوج], **Ma'lūj** [معلوج], **Ṭaṭlūkh** [ططلوخ], **Hal** [هل], **Hakayūka'** [هكيوكع], **Maklīl** [مكليل], **Namūh** [نموه], **Yāh** [ياه], **Yāh** [ياه]. **'Thereafter it becomes dry stubble that the winds scatter.' God**

indeed has power over all things. By Aymāsh [ايماش], **Shayūsh** [شيوش], **Ṭaylā** [طيلا], **Laṭūsh** [لطوش], **Shakam** [شكم], **Shakam** [شكم]. **Incinerate him, O friends of the Lord. That is the command of the Creator, which He has revealed unto you.**

This completes the seven planetary seals. Success is through God.

The Seal Of The Twelve Hosts Who Descended With Iblis On The Day Of His Fall From Grace

This is a noble seal of tremendous obedience and speedy compliance, which you can employ in all works of piety. Seven spiritual angels, twelve servants, and four ifreet, who are in charge of the carpet of the seal, are attached to it.

If you wish to make it, prepare yourself and, with the blessing of the Lord and His good aid, fashion a ring from pure silver if possible, otherwise out of brass, according to the number of planets. Inscribe it on Friday or Sunday, during the first hour. After inscribing it, wash it with running water and salt, make a red bag for it,

and elevate it until you set it out under the stars in the prescribed manner. This is the greatest and most exalted of them, as it is of tremendous obedience and high status. It has a number of the Ruhaniyyah and Rebels that only God, Mighty and Majestic, can enumerate. You can employ it, by the permission of the Divine, for all things you need and all the real previously mentioned operations. It is the seal of the twelve hosts who descended with Iblis. The sage Ma'adaryus said: "I asked the Perfect Nature about the Seal of the Regions and he said, 'The Great Hermes told me that the Unifier, that is, the Seal of the Twelve Hosts, was in the possession of Tabarin al-Hindi, king of India, who was a believing man. Asaph the son of Berechiah said, "Tabarin, king of India, was the first to pledge allegiance to Solomon the son of David."' I asked which seal is easier and more beneficial and he said, 'Stick to the Seal of the Regions, which is the Unifier obeyed by all the kings, for the scholars have not produced a seal better than it.'" Moreover, it is the seal of Ma'adaryus. The jinn used to attend his assembly because therein was the Creator's Greatest Name, with which He created all the planets.

The Names Of Iblis' Aides

Answer, O Jarīr [جرير]; O Khandash [خندش]; O Khaydash [خيدش]; O Naykal; O Asyaf [اسيف] the Swordsman; O Rūqīl [روقيل] of Rafīq [رفيق]; O Sa'dūn [سعدون], master of the shackles; O Marhayā [مرهيا], master of the fortresses; O Yaqṭaṭarūn [يقططرون], master of the deep prison; O Alhūtak [الهوتك] the Greatest; O Mazkakayūn [مزككيون], resident of the horizons.

Simmah ibn Das al-Hindi said: "I asked the Perfect Nature about the seal, how to make it, and how to use it, and he said, 'O my son, I have not grown weary since the day it fell into my hands! It is knowledge the scholars have concealed from the ignorant and therefore I entrusted it to the Great Hermes.' He also said to me, 'You shall write it in gold on white crystal, or in gold on pure silver. Its operation shall be on Friday, when its planet is in its exaltation, or on any day you wish, provided its planet is in its exaltation. When its inscription is finished, wash it with running water and salt and place it in a red silk

bag. It should be set out under the stars in the first week of the Arabic month, when the new Moon is fortunate, and it should be hung by a red silk thread between three branches of a pomegranate tree or, if possible, a quince tree. This should take place in a clean house remote from inhabitation: it should take place in the house in the daytime and at night when the stars are emerging. You should conjure him three times at night and three times in the day—the beginning, middle, and end of it. Cover yourself with amulets, and surround yourself therewith, not for fear of him but of others (aerial and terrestrial jinn will gather round it). If you are able and have endurance to stay awake at night and recite the conjuration, you should recite the conjuration from the start of the night to its end, for this will hasten the response and intensify obedience. You should fast in the daytime and stay awake at night, praying; sleep not unless it overcomes you. At the end of your speech you should say, "Answer by the leave of the Lord, O company of seven kings." On the fourth night, you will hear their words, but fear not, for on the fifth night, your sight will become unveiled and you will see them standing before you. On the seventh night, they will speak to you and request from you their conditions; impose on them whatever conditions you wish and request from each king an aide to serve you in addition to what you have. When that happens to you, your seal will be complete, with your operation sound, your power complete, and your command and prohibition obeyed. Therefore, be righteous as commanded, pursue the pleasure of your Lord, and commit not what He has forbidden, for you have arrived by the power of your Master. Do not entreat anyone besides Him, or be heedless of your devotion to Him, for to Him is your end. Furthermore, He has granted you your petition, so do not anull your work and become one of the losers." The usage and benefits of this seal will come, God Most High willing, in the chapter "The Usage of the Seals and the Carpet." Seek help from the Divine, and trust in Him.'

The Conjuration for The Twelve Hosts' Seal

After the spiritual conjuration, which begins with "In the name of Him by whose command the heavens exist," say: I entreat you, O company of pure spirits obedient unto God, Lord of the Worlds, from among all spiritual beings, by the right of these names, to hear my call and make haste to reply: you, O Mahmayā'īl [مهميائيل], and you, O Ṭaḥīṭamyā'īl [طحيطميائيل], and you, O Sarā'īl [سرائيل], and you, O Marqayā'īl [مرقيائيل], and you, O 'Arnayā'īl [عرنيائيل], and you, O Bāhil [باهل], and you, O Nūrā'īl [نوراعيل], by the right

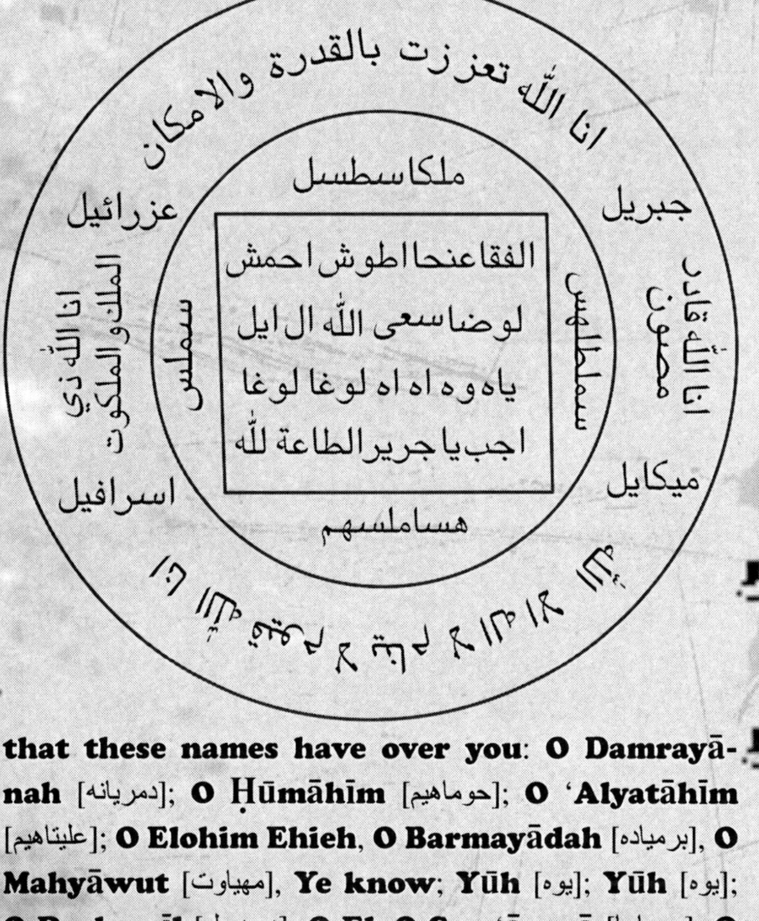

that these names have over you: **O Damrayā-nah** [دمريانه]; **O Ḥūmāhīm** [حوماهيم]; **O ʻAlyatāhīm** [عليتاهيم]; **O Elohim Ehieh**, **O Barmayādah** [برمياده], **O Mahyāwut** [مهياوت], **Ye know**; **Yūh** [يوه]; **Yūh** [يوه]; **O Darhawīl** [درهويل]; **O El**; **O Samʻāyayā** [سمعاييا]; **O He who is transcendent and therefore cannot be seen**, **Who is above the uppermost firmaments**, **Who gives death unto to the living and life unto the dead**, **Who knows that which is secret and yet more hidden**. **Haste ye by the right of these names**: **O ʻĀliyā** [عاليا], **Bakyā** [بكيا], **Hayāh** [هياه], **Yāh** [ياه], **Yāh** [ياه], **Yāh** [ياه], **Mahyālāyā** [مهياليا], **Atbāṭ** [اتباط], **Nayāyā** [نيايا], **Ehieh Asher Ehieh**. **I ask You by the greatness of Your power**: **I ask You to as-**

sist me with these hosts by Your might, and to subordinate unto me Your angels Shamlīkhiyā [شمليخيا], **Mūṭaṭmayakh** [موططميخ], **Tataḥlayā** [تتحليا], **Khafakh** [خفخ], **Sarmīl** [سرميل], **Mahramīkh** [مهرميخ], **Batmalīkhā** [بتمليخا], **Ṭamyaṭakhyā** [طميطخيا], **Marīkh** [مريخ], **Baṭīkh** [بطيخ], **Rakūr** [ركور], **Kūḥayat** [كوحيت], **'Ayat** [عيت], **Hayat** [هيت], **Ṭalshīkh** [طلشيخ], **Ṭaṭīkh** [ططيخ], **Ḥayjar** [حيجر], **Marīl** [مريل], **Hūjal** [هوجل], **and Amīkh** [اميخ]. **Answer me, O company of hosts, by Manjām** [منجام], **Hamyah** [هميه], **Manjalmah** [منجلمه], **Yā Ni'mah** [نعمة], **Jalam** [جلم], **Asaylashīsh** [اسيلشيش], **El, El, (glorious is He and highly exalted), Astahrab** [استهرب], **Astahrab** [استهرب], **Shamhayamūkh** [شمهيموخ], **Mastaṭū** [مستطو], **Walā** [ولا], **Mīd** [ميد], **Qudrah** [قدرة], **Fayashtāṭūsh** [فيشتاطوش], **Kāf Hā Yā 'Ayn Ṣād** [كهيعص], **Mastās** [مستاس], **Abaryashāwub** [ابريشاوب], **'Āṣa'ṣa'ā** [عاصعصعا], **al-Ḥayy** [الحي], **al-Qayyūm** [القيوم], **Masayrahā** [مسيرها], **Qudrah** [قدرة], **Qudrah** [قدرة]. **Obedience unto Allah, by Shayādayūh** [شياديوه], **Nāyūh** [نايوه], **Majrabīlā** [مجربيلا], **Mastasnamūh** [مستسنموه], **Sahūh** [سهوه], **Istaqṭar** [استقطر], **Fayrīk** [فيريك], **Nūrak** [نورك], **Saba'ūd** [سبعود], **Mastās** [مستاس], **Rabb** [رب], **Anūt** [انوت], **Ḥā Mīm 'Ayn Sīn Qāf** [حم عسق], **Saṭawūn** [سطوون], **al-Musayṭirūn** [مسيطرون]. **That is God, my Lord, Who has no partner.**

The Second Conjuration for the Twelve Hosts' Seal

After the first, say: The Most Glorious, The Most Holy, Lord of the angels and the Spirit. Glory be unto the Creator of light, Sayla‘ [سيلع], **Yaka‘** [يكع]; **Lāh** [لاه]; **Darṭamīnā** [درطمينا]; **Yā Rayā** [يا ريا]; **Yā Marnītā** [مرنيتا]—**hurry**!— **Adonai; El Shaddi; Hatamūtah** [هتموته]; **‘Alaq** [علق]; **Mayhāyir** [ميهاير]; **Bahar** [بهر]; **Hū** [هو]; **Kāf Hā Yā ‘Ayn Ṣād** [كهيعص]; **Ḥā Mīm ‘Ayn Sīn Qāf** [حم عسق]; **Ehieh Asher Ehieh; by Sa‘sīm** [سعسيم]; **‘Ayū** [عيو]; **Hayhūb** [هيهوب]; **Malūfīsh** [ملوفيش]; **Athīnāl** [اثينال]; **Hayhayā** [هيهيا]; **by Ṭūṭayāl** [طوطيال]; **Ṭa‘laṭ** [طعلط]; **Laṭlaṭ** [لطلط]. **All that is in the heavens and the earth glorify Him, willingly or unwillingly, and unto Him you will be returned. Answer by the bright fire and the piercing flame, O company of servants; by Ta‘ṭayā‘īl** [تعطيائيل], **Namūh** [نموه], **Adzahīd** [ادزهيد], **Hūh** [هوه], **Qad** [قد], **Khatīthā** [ختيثا], **Arṭashūsh** [ارطشوش], **Ṭayṭakhūsh** [طيطخوش], **Namūh** [نموه], **Ṭayṭakhākhūsh** [طيطخاخوش], **Namūh** [نموه], **El, El. Obedience unto the Lord, O company of angels, by the right of Him who said unto the heavens**

and the earth, 'Come willingly or unwillingly,' to which they replied, 'We shall come willingly.' Likewise come unto me obediently and quickly, by the honor of the Lord of the Worlds.

Conjuration to the Four Ifreets

These are the ones in charge of the signet ring, plus their seal, their secret, and their subjugation.

You say: O Barākh [براخ], **Barākh** [براخ], **Ashnaydayān** [اشنيديان], **Ashnaydayān** [اشنيديان], **Matraʿān** [مترعان], **Jayāsh** [جياش], **Jayāsh** [جياش], **Qaṭrayūsh** [قطريوش], **Abham** [ابهم], **Ṭūhūm** [طوهوم], **Shālikh** [شالخ]. **Hurry, O wings of the cherubim and glorification of the Spiritual Ones, by the glory of El, the One, the Subduer, who does as He wills. Make haste, O Maymūn** [ميمون], **O Mīṭaṭrūn** [ميططرون], **O Ḥālīsh** [حاليش], **O Majlīsh** [مجليش]; **answer by the honor of the One, the Triumphant, Who does as He pleases.**

Instructions for the Seal of Mahakil and Sakhr

Ṣakhr is Ṣakhr ibn 'Amr ibn Shujil ibn al-Abyadh ibn Ḥamlit al-Jinni. He has a number of rebel jinn that only Allah, Glorious and Exalted, can enumerate. For him, fashion a ring from pure silver with a carnelian stone, on either Sunday or Friday, when their planets are in their exaltations, and inscribe it. When you have completed its inscription, wash it in rose water with musk and camphor dissolved in it. Thereafter, set it out under the stars in the prescribed manner.

The following is the seal:

دا ک ا ه ا ▽ ا ر ٦ ▽ ط ه ط ه ع رالط
ا د ا ح ا٨ ح اا اا ٨ ا ر ح هساكيل
كصل ك وا ٦ ا رر اا مـــر و
٢ ه ٦ ٦ ا٧ ٨ ااا ا ط ااا رلو ااوى
اجب يا مهاكيل

All of the Seven Kings are obliged to obey it.

Say: **Answer**, **O Mahākīl** [مهاكيل], **and you**, **O Ḥūq** [حوق], **and you**, **O Ṣāliḥ** [صالح], **and you**, **O Sulaymān** [سليمان], **and you**, **O progeny of Ṣakhr** [صخر], **by the right of the names and the seals that encircle you and all the Seven Kings**. **Come obediently**, **by the leave of the Lord of the Worlds**.

You write that (**starting from your words**, **Answer**, **O Mahakil**, **and you**, **O Huq**... **to the end of it**) **below the seal**.

Conjuration To The Progeny Of Sakhr And All Of The Seven Kings

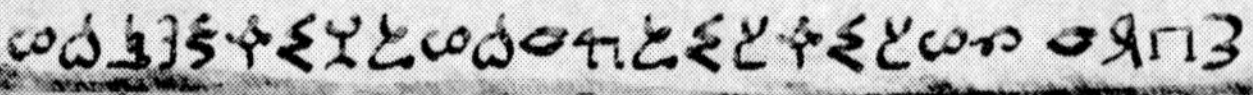

Say these on important occassions. **Those whom you call will answer collectively**, **if you wish**, **or individually**; **if you wish**, **you can separate them**, **and if you wish**, **you can bring them together**. **You say**: **El**; **El**; **Zaḥāj** [زحاج]; **by Za'rah** [زعرة]; **El**; **Aḥmad** [احمد]; **Rīkh** [ريخ]; **Alṭūd** [الطود]; **Ṭūd** [طود]; **Aṭal** [اطل]; **Yāligh** [يالغ]; **Lafārakrā** [لفاركرا]; **Sham** [شم]; **Lā** [لا]; **Bīgh** [بيغ]; **Raqash** [رقش]; **Yādah** [ياده]; **Shāmīn** [شامين]; **Tham** [ثم]; **Akban** [اكبن]. **Answer**, **O company of seven kings**, **by the right**

that these noble and magnificent names have over you.

Instructions For Sakhr's Seal

He is an Aide over whom Solomon the son of David was empowered, and he is the master of the Mandal.

Fashion a ring from copper or gold, if that is possible, otherwise out of carnelian, which is better. Do this on either Sunday or on Thursday, when the planets of either day are in their exaltations. Inscribe the seal on it, or on something similar to it, on Friday, at the start of the Arabic month. After inscribing it, wash it with running water and salt and set it out under the stars in the prescribed manner.

Thereafter, cense it with aloeswood and storax and place it in a clean bag in a high place. The following is the blessed seal, just as you see it:

اا ا ط اهـ ا ⊠ ا ∩ اه ا ٨ ا اااا
٤ اا ٨ هـ ااا اهلـك اا عـــس
اا ٩ اا ⊠ ٨ اااا ا ٦ ا ٩ ⩘ ااك
ک اساط ے ٢ طمن اجب ياصخر

First Conjuration of Mahakil [مهاكيل], The Guardian of Solomon's Mandal

It is as follows. Say: A conjuration from the Creator and His messenger unto every obstinate tyrant and rebellious devil of watery, airy, earthy, and fiery nature. By the right that these names have over you, I conjure you to answer my call, hasten my reply, obey the names of the Lord Most High, and fulfill my need. Hurry, hurry, hurry, hurry, by the right which these names hold over you: 'Tamūh [تموه]; Shaqshaqah

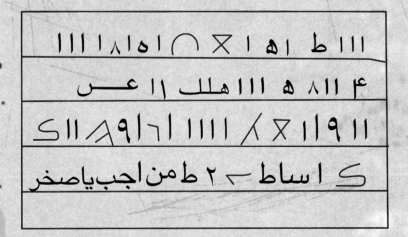

[شقشقه]; **Namūh** [نموه]; **Lahūh** [لهوه]; **by Nawā** [نوا], **Nawā** [نوا]; **Tūdūh** [تودوه]; **Barābar** [برابر]; **Kashī** [كشي], **Kashī** [كشي]; **Ajrazakshī** [اجرزكشي]; **Karbah** [كربه]; **Aqrāh** [اقراة]; **Hūhah** [هوهه]; **Tamūyanah** [تموينه]; **Yajafrashah** [يجفرشه]; **Sahā'īk** [سهائيك]; **Shafāhā** [شفاها], **Shafāhā** [شفاها].' **Answer ye**, **obedient unto the command of God**, **hastening unto His names**. **Answer you**!

Second Conjuration Of Mahakil

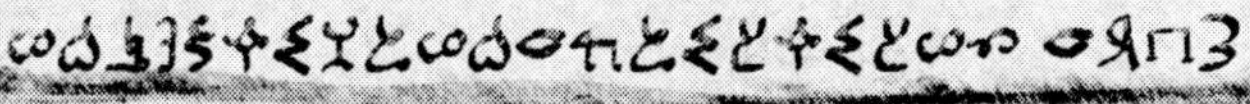

Say: **Aynabalīsh** [اينبليش], **El**, **El**, **Ayn** [اين], **Mahākīl** [مهاكيل], **Mahākīlā** [مهاكيلا], **Kīsh** [كيش], **Kīsh** [كيش], **Falīsh** [فليش], **Yatba'** [يتبع], **Tatah** [تته], **Mahākīl** [مهاكيل], **Shalahīshah** [شلهيشه]. **Obedience is unto the Lord and His names**, **O Mahākīl** [مهاكيل]. **Answer you**!

Third Conjuration Of Mahakil

Say: **Qahūshah** [قهوشه], **Shahāhah** [شهاهة], **Māyah** [ماية], **Madh-hanah** [مذهنه], **Yad-hashah** [يدهشه], **Sharhalah** [شرهله], **Shafāhah** [شفاهة], **Bakrah** [بكره], **Bakrah** [بكره], **Shajrah** [شجره], **Ṣaḥāṣaḥā** [صحاصحا], **Nahāhah** [نهاهه], **Shalamū‘** [شلموع]. **Answer obediently**, **O Mahākīl** [مهاكيل].

Fourth Conjuration Of Mahakil

Say: **Anhādah** [انهاده]; **Hayhādah** [هيهاده]; **Shahāshah** [شهاشه]; **Marāniyah** [مرانيه]; **by Karsha‘ah** [كرشعة]; **Sharsha‘ah** [شرشعه];

Shafāhā [شفاها]; Shafāhā [شفاها]; Shafāhah [شفاهة]; Waṭāyah [وطاية]; Jazahah [جزهة]. Make haste, O company of angels. Come unto me, all together, obedient unto the command of God Most Great, hastily, whether male or female, O Banū Ṣakhr [بنو صخر], O Banū Dāhir [بنو داهر], and O Banū 'Amr [بنو عمر].

If the Kings delay, inscribe the seal of Ṣakhr [صخر] on iron or copper and bring it near the heat of a fire and they will come to you quicker than the flash of lightning. This completes the conjurations.

Illustration of the Mandal of Solomon

Also, (concerning) its uses, real operations for healing and the like that are needed, and the conjuring all the celestial and terrestrial ruhaniyyah.

This is one of the hidden secrets of Solomon (peace be upon him). Inscribe the following symbol on silver, if you are able to, otherwise

on copper whitened with naphtha. Thereafter, set it out under the stars with the two previous seals (the seal of Ṣakhr [صخر] and the seal of Mahākīl [مهاكيل]) in the prescribed manner. This is the symbol:

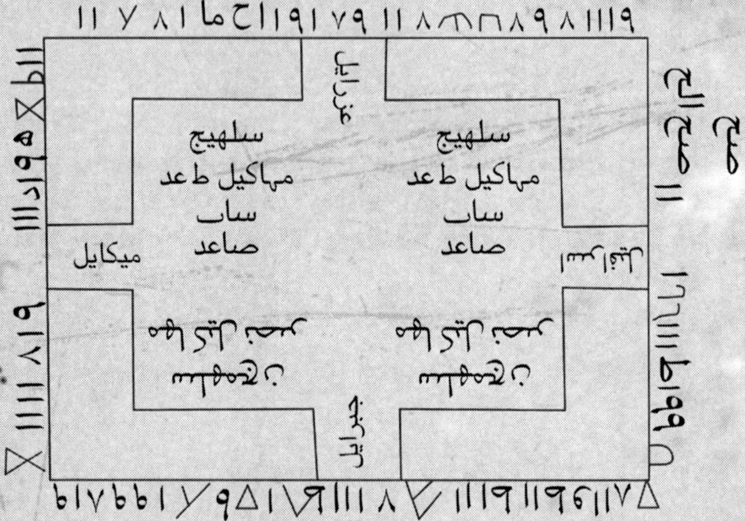

If you cannot find such metals, inscribe it on clean earth. Moreover, you must raise the seals above the ground upon four pedestals.

Solomon's Mandal, on which all the spirits forcibly descended with obedience, served as the design for this noble Mandal.

If someone brings a Wind-afflicted person to you, and you wish to use it, summon Mahākīl [مهاكيل], bring the afflicted person inside the Mandal, and order him as you wish. In addition, write the Names of Seership between the friend's eyes and command him to look at his companion in the Mandal. When he sees him, know that his body is free of the Wind. With that, equip him with amulets, and either have the Wind swear a covenant with you concerning the victim, imprison him, or kill him. But do not hasten to kill him, for a rebellious jinni, whether Muslim or non-Muslim, must violate the covenant three times before being killed.

The mandal has a number of uses that none but God Most High can enumerate. Among its wondrous properties are the following: If you desire someone, be he near or far, prestigious or otherwise, then make an effigy of him and stand it in the center of the Mandal. If it is daytime, encircle it with seven banners, each in a different color, attached to seven cubit-long spears. If it is nighttime, encircle it with seven lit candles on seven banners. Thereafter recite the four conjurations and summon the one you wish and, even if he is across the seven seas, this will bring him instantly, for heed of, and out of obedience to, God Most High and His names. If you wish to annihilate someone, then, after placing a belonging of his or something containing his perspiration inside the Mandal, stand his effigy therein and command as you wish concerning him and it will be done. Be cautious of doing this, and only do it for that which will incur the favor of the Lord Most High upon you. If someone brings a Wind-afflicted person to you, and you wish to burn the Wind inside his body, write the following names in a bowl, wash it off, and then give it to him to drink and the Wind will be burned in his body.

These are the names: **Fāṭir** [فاطر]; **Raqah** [رقه]; **Amsā** [امسا]; **Amsā** [امسا] ; **Dāwā** [داوا]; **'Atah** [عته]; **Kaslaṭī** [كسلطي]; **by 'Alam** [علم]; **Shansarūdan** [شنسرودن]; **Wadad** [ودد], **by Shaymas** [شيمس]. **Burn**, **by the leave of the Lord Most Magnificent**! **'And had We willed**, **We could have transfixed them where they stood**, **so they could move neither forward nor backwards**.**' Answer you and burn**!

The Names of Seership, Which You Write Between the Eyes of the Possessed

They are as follows: **Alfarqash** [الفرقش], **Hāmūr** [هامور], **Asar** [اسر]. **Look**, **by the right of Shakhmalūsh** [شخملوش], **Salahā** [سلها], **Ṭaysh** [طيش], **Ṭayshīsh** [طيشيش], **Haṭīsh** [هطيش], **Armīsh** [ارميش]. **Look**, **by the right of Shakhmalūsh** [شخملوش].

If a jinni defies you, **and you wish him to remain in your presence so you can command him as you please**, **write the following names on a piece of paper and fix it to the soles of his feet and he will not be able to leave**, **even if one year passes**,

until you release him:

The Manner of the Jinn Covenant

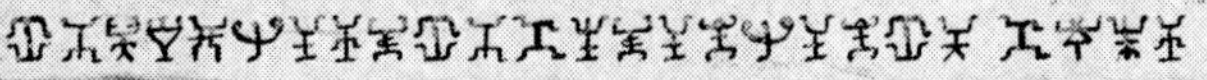

Say to the possessing jinni: Swear a covenant by the Lord, besides whom there is no god, Knower of the unseen and seen, the Triumphant, the Omnipotent, Who watches over every soul and knows what it earns, by Whose command the heavens and the earth stand, that you shall never again return unto this human, neither when he is awake, nor when he is sleep, nor in the night, nor in the day, and that if you should return, you will be worthy of death.

Repeat that three times so the Kings hear it, then write the following: 'The Divine One testifies that there is no god but Him, and so do the angels and those endowed with knowledge, standing firm upon justice. There is no god but Him, Almighty and Wise.' Those endowed with

knowledge, the Kings, and all present at the covenant of the jinn N. the son of N. (you ask him his name), testify that if he should return to this body or draw near it, then he has disobeyed God and therefore deserves death.

Thereafter, write the following covenant, which is for all the jinn, along with an amulet, and hang it around his neck:

ر ط ط ط ح ▽ ‖ ١ ▽ ∧ ١

ر ط ط ط ح ▽ ‖ ١ G ٥ ٩ ‖ ک ٥

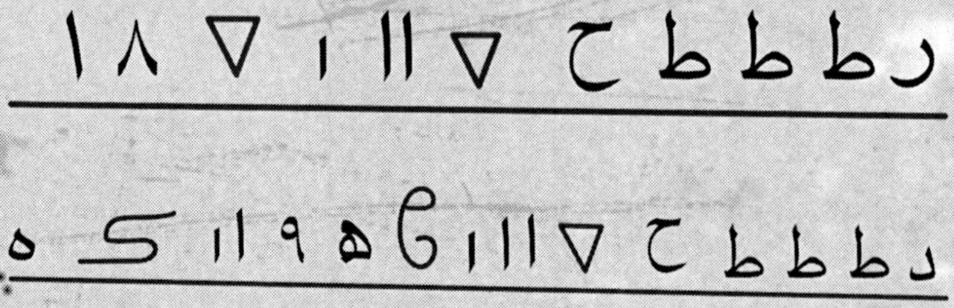

Asaph the son of Berechiah said, "If you wish to kill an oppressive opponent or rebel, draw a figure of him and encircle it so that everything other than its hands is in the circle. Then write the following names on its belly and command as you wish. If you insert something into the belly of the figure, it will be inserted into the belly of the rebel. These are the names: Ṭayṭalahūsh [طيطلهوش], Hashar [هشر], Malī' [مليع], Naqfan [نقفن], Ṭahṭalayūsh [طهطليوش], Ṭaṭrash [ططرش], Haka' [هكع], Haya' [هيع], Ṭalīkh [طليخ], Ṭafṭīkh [طفطيخ].

Instructions for Maymun Aba Nukh's Obedience Compelling Spear

Make a plate from steel on Saturday, during the hour of Saturn, when Libra is on the ascendent, and during this hour, or in one similar to it on another day, inscribe it. Thereafter wash it with running water and salt, make a cover for it, and set it out under the stars with any of the seals.

Inscribe the first side of it with these names: O company! Ṣarṣar **al- Muṣayṣir** [صرصر المصيصر]; **Jalshar** [جلشر]; ‘**Araqūshah** [عرقوشة]; **Naṭfa‘af** [نطفعف]; **Kaylah** [كيله]; **Kayrab** [كيرب]; **Ashayṣa‘ūn** [اشيصعون]; **Wakarīkh** [وكريخ]; **Mayhar** [ميهر]; **Layṭaraq** [ليطرق]; **Mar‘a‘ar** [مرععر]; ‘Ānī [عانى]; **O Qarṣaṣā** [قرصصا]; **O Bahaljayū** [بهلجيو]; **Fashā** [فشا]; **Bashahūkhayā** [بشهوخيا]; **O Ṭaybar** [طيبر]; **Layhalāqah** [ليهلاقه]; **Ba‘lamī** [بعلمي]; **Fulā** [فلا]; **Yamā** [يوما]; **Lūtayā** [لوتيا]. **Obedient ones, answer by the power of the Divine**.

Inscribe the following on the first side of the hilt: Rebuke, O Maymūn [ميمون], **by Ehieh Asher**

Ehieh, **El Shaddi**, **Tzabaoth**, **Bayrā** [بيرا], **Ṭabara‘** [طبرع], **‘Alshāqish** [علشاقش], **Mahrāqish** [مهراقش], **Aqshābaqash** [اقشابقش], **Shaqamū** [شقمو], **Nahshar** [نهشر], **Kashālikh** [كشالخ], **‘Aqshar** [عقشر], **Ṭahash** [طهش].

Inscribe the following on the second side of the hilt: **Subbūḥ** [سبوح], **Subbūḥ** [سبوح], **Quddūs** [قدوس], **Lord of the angels and the Spirit**. **Glory be unto the Creator of light**, **Sahla‘anka‘** [سهلعنكع], **Lā** [لا], Ūr**aḥmatā** [اورحمتا], **Bāriyā** [باريا], **Marehītā** [مرثيتا]. **Make haste**, **O Ṭayyib** [طيب].

Instructions For Maymun's Athame

When the previously mentioned sign of the zodiac is on the ascendent, **inscribe the following on one side of the blade**:

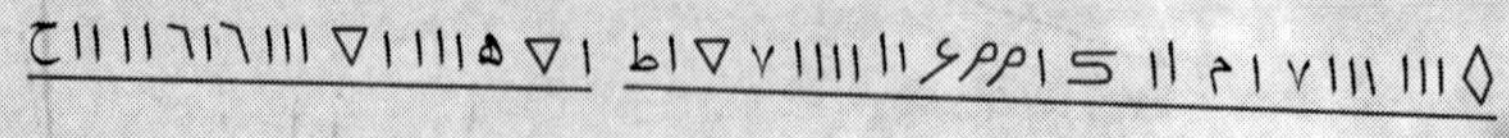

Inscribe the following on the other side:

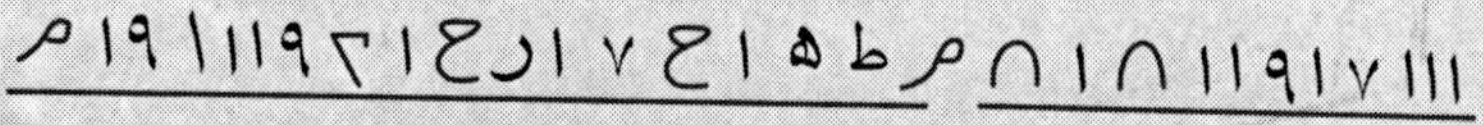

On the handle, inscribe the following along with Maymūn's [ميمون] **Names of Killing**: **Jibrīl** [جبريل], **Mīkā'īl** [ميكائيل], **Isrāfīl** [إسرافيل], **Hanfalat** [هنفلت], **Adonai Tzabaoth**.

Thereafter, draw the image of the Mandal on a clean floor, write the following names on a piece of paper or on the floor, insert the knife into any letter you wish, and say, "O Maymūn [ميمون], **kill him!" and he will kill him. Alternatively, if you cut the paper with scissors, he will be cut in a like manner. These are the names**: **By Ṭaṭarūyash** [ططرويش], **Hash** [هش], **Malba'** [ملبع], **La'fī** [لعفى], **Ṭafṭūsh** [طفطوش], **Ṭahṭalayūsh** [طهطليوش], **Maḥkamīh** [محكميه], **Ṭakhīkh** [طخيخ], **Ḥaj** [حج], **Ḥajīj** [حجيج], **Qaẓā** [قظا], **'Alayṭā** [عليطا], **Saqṭamā** [سقطما].

If a King or possessing jinni rebels against you, and you wish to kill him, write the following names on a piece of paper, if possible, otherwise on the floor. Then stab it with the athame of Maymūn [ميمون] **(whatever you do to it will be done to him). Moreover, summon any King you wish and he will obey your command. They are as follows**: **Ṭamṭamlosh** [طمطملوش]

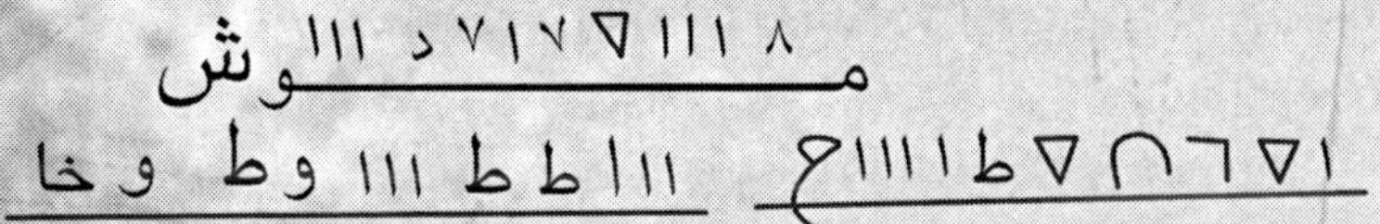

The Names on Abu al-Walīd Shamhurash's [أبو وليد شمهورش] Athame

Inscribe them onto iron on Thursday, when Jupiter is in its exaltation. You inscribe one side with this line:

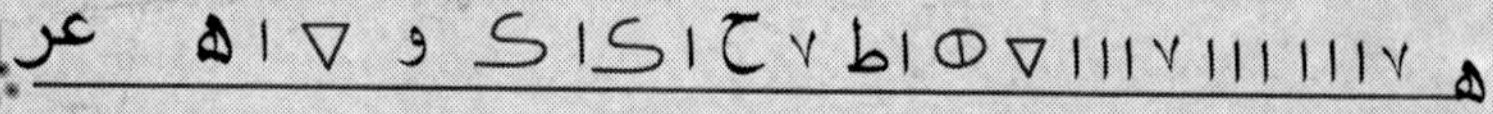

Inscribe the other side with these:

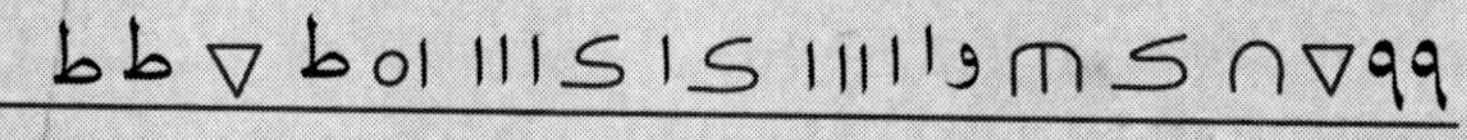

Halshalshalīkh [هلشلشليخ], **Halmashīkh** [هلمشيخ], **Malshakīkh** [ملشكيخ], **Alsa'ālīn** [السعالين], **Matatīhā** [متطيها], **Bātāmūn** [باتامون]. **O Kāmūn Aghaythā** [كامون اغيثا], **by Yā, Yā, Hūmīn** [هومين], **Hawāmīr** [هوامير]. **O Nawāmīr** [نوامير] **of the Flames**! **O master of the Khawātif** [خواطف]!

Inscribe the handle with the following: **Jibrīl** [جبريل], **Mīkā'īl** [ميكائيل], **Isrāfīl** [إسرافيل]. **By Khalkhamash** [خلخمش], **Khanjamīsh** [خنجميش], **Ja'jamīsh** [جعجعميش], **Ja'jamīsh** [جعجعميش], **Akmash** [اكمش], **Makīsh** [مكيش], **Kalamīsh** [كلميش], **Kalamīsh**

[كلميش], **Yakash** [يكش], **Saḥaq** [سحق], **Saḥaq** [سحق], **Shalash** [شلش], **Ṭaqash** [طقش], **Mafūsh** [مفوش], **Fakūsh** [فكوش]. **I destroy ye, O enemy of the Creator, by the 'kindled fire of the Lord that reaches unto the heavens. Verily it will be closed over them.' And I burn you by Halmashīkh** [هلمشيخ], **Malshakīkh** [ملشكيخ], **Alsa'ālīn** [السعالين], **Mataṭīhā** [متطيها], **Bātāmūn** [باتامون]. **O Kāmūn Aghaythā** [كامون اغيثا], **by Yā, Yā, Hūmīn** [هومين], **Hawāmīr** [هوامير]. **O Nawāmīr** [نوامير] **of the Flames! O master of the Khawāṭif** [خواطف]!

Know that these names are of potent obedience and speedy response. The following are some of the wonders of their properties: If you wish to expel a Wind from a person's body, then write the following line where the Wind is, and also on a tablet or piece of wood or, as a last resort, a clean floor. Then, as you recite the names, stab the letters in the line, one by one, until the Wind exits the body. Below is an illustration of the line; guard it, for it is one of the great secrets. It is as follows:

The Seal Of Khandash [خندش] And Naykal [نيكل]

The two brothers of al-Aḥmar [الأحمر] are independent kings and thus owe no obedience to any king. They also were the two headsmen of Solomon the son of David. You can employ them for anything, whether great or small.

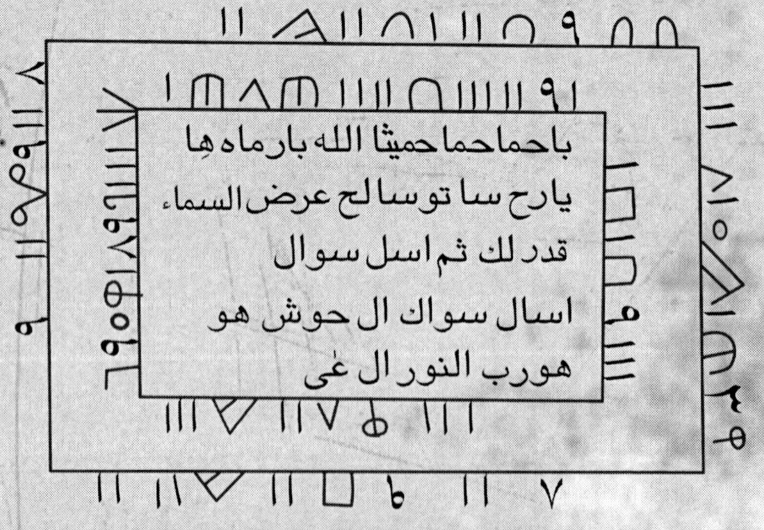

If you wish to do that, inscribe a copper ring on the first Tuesday of a lunar month, during the hour of Mars, when Capricorn is on the ascendant. After you inscribe it, wash it with water

and salt, make a red bag for it, and set it out under the stars for seven nights.

Say: Answer, O Khandash [خندش], **and you, O Naykal** [نيكل]. **Then call out the names of the Aides. Say: Answer, O Najāḥ** [نجاح], **and you, O Aflaḥ** [أفلح], **and you, O Abū al-Akhwaṣ** [أبو الأخوص]. **Following is a conjuration to him. Say: Taghmārish** [تغمارش], **Taghmārish** [تغمارش], **Tarash** [ترش], **Tarear** [ترتر], **Harhar** [هرهر], **Marmar** [مرمر], **Qazqaz** [قزقز], **Yūsh** [يوش], **Yūsh** [يوش], **Janā** [جنا], **Janūsh** [جنوش], **Ṭālaythā** [طاليثا], **Athāthā** [اثاثا], **Athāthā** [اثاثا], **Hāhah** [هاهه], **Hāhah** [هاهه], **Hāhā** [هاها], **Hāhayah** [هاهيه], **'Ashlash** [عشلش], **'Ashlash** [عشلش], **Aqya'** [اقيع], **Aqya'** [اقيع], **Yārikh** [يارخ], **Yārikh** [يارخ], **Taythā** [تيثا], **Būthālikh** [بوثالخ], **Aḥmā** [احما], **Ḥamaythā** [حميثا], **Bāriyā** [باريا], **Mūthaythā** [موثيثا], **Al'arūb** [العروب], **Shalakh** [شلخ], **Faklā** [فكلا], **Fashūf** [فشوف], **Almīl** [الميل], **Faqṭalash** [فقطلش], **Hanfād** [هنفاد], **Akhaythā** [اخيثا], **Ah** [اه], **Ah** [اه], **Ḥamā** [حما], **Ḥamaythā** [حميثا]. **The Creator proportioned you, then makes the way easy for you. Answer by the right of 'Azīz 'Az 'Alṭaf** [عزيز عز علطف]. **O Baylakh** [بيلخ], **respond by the right of Mīṭaṭrūn** [ميططرون] **and Makhlayā'īl** [مخليائيل], **Qadūf** [قدوف], **Qadūf** [قدوف], **Alūrahūd** [الورهود], **Daqūshayā** [دقوشيا], **Amaylā** [اميلا], **Amaylā** [اميلا], **Wakhabīlā** [وخبيلا], **Lūshā** [لوشا], **Darbīlā** [دربيلا], **Za'bīlā** [زعبيلا]. **Hurry, O Khandash** [خندش] **and Naykal** [نيكل], **by Damlākh** [دملاخ], **Damlākh** [دملاخ], **Barākh** [براخ], **Barākh** [براخ], **Jūlā** [جولا], **Hīlā** [هيلا], **Shamlā** [شملا], **Shaṭāf** [شطاف], **Ṣafīf** [صفيف], **Maṭūf** [مطوف], **Khaṭāf**

[خطاف], **Ṭāyif** [طايف], **Shaqdayāsh** [شقدياش], **Shaqdayāsh** [شقدياش], **Jawfashām** [جوفشام], **Mayūlā** [ميولا], **Mayūlā** [ميولا], **Shaṭālish** [شطالش], **Haylawān** [هيلوان], **Mayṭarīsh** [ميطريش]. **'How should we not put our trust in the Lord, when He has guided us in our ways? We will surely endure your persecution of us. Let the believers put their trust in God.' Answer me, O Khandash** [خندش], **and you, O Naykal** [نيكل], **and you, O Najāḥ** [نجاح], **and you, O Aflaḥ** [أفلح], **and you, O Abū al-Akhwaṣ** [أبو الأخوص], **by the power of the Lord of power.**

Instructions for the Seal of Abu Ma'bad Zunbur [أبو معبد زنبور], Master of Illusions

With the aid of God Most High, make a ring out of either seven or three metals: gold, silver, porcelain [ed: included as a replacement for Mercury], tin, lead, copper, and iron. Do this on Thursday, during the hour of Jupiter. Inscribe it when this planet is in its exaltation. Then wash it with water and salt, make a yellow bag for it, and elevate it until you set it out under the stars in the prescribed manner. The following is the seal, just as you see it:

You say: **I conjure thee**, **O Abū Ma'bad Zunbūr** [[أبو معبد زنبور], **by that by which the Creator swore unto the heavens and the earth**, **by 'Aṭyahūsh** [عطيهوش], **Manṭahūsh** [منطهوش], **Ayā** [أيا], **Hayṭash** [هيطش], **Qasyāqūsh** [قسياقوش], **Maharūyash** [مهرويش], **Shalāshalā** [شلاشلا], **Halā** [هلا], **Halā** [هلا]. **Exalted is Matāhūtā** [متاهوتا]. **'And they said**, **"We hear and obey**. **Your forgiveness we seek**, **O Lord**, **and unto You is the end**."' **Ḥalash** [حلش], **Mafāṭir** [مفاطر], **Aṭarīsh** [اطريش], **Dahash** [دهش], **Nahash** [نهش], **Qamahmahat** [قمهمهت], **Bahamīsh** [بهميش], **Bashārah** [بشاره], **Manshayah** [منشيه]. **Hurry**! **Hurry**! **'It is**

from Solomon, and it is in the name of God, Most Merciful and Compassionate. "Be not arrogant towards me, but come ye unto me, subservient."' Yaqlaqash [يقلقش], **Qūnūsh** [قونوش], **Darmūsh** [درموش], **Halāhayūsh** [هلاهيوش], **Fahnadūyash** [فهندويش], **Hayṭalīlakh** [هيطليلخ]. **Answer me, O Abū Ma'bad Zunbūr** [أبو معبد زنبور], **by the name by which our Lord sends down rain and causes water to come forth from the stones, and by the name by which He will resurrect the dead, whereupon the soul will return unto the body. In whatsoever part of the earth ye may be, whether its plains, badlands, mainland, or seas, 'The Lord will bring you all together; surely He has power over all things.' Hasten, O Abū Ma'bad Zunbūr** [أبو معبد زنبور], **and answer me by that with which I have conjured ye, and by Him who says unto a thing 'Be!' whereupon it is.**

Second Conjuration To Abu Ma'bad Zunbur

Y ousay: **Adam**[ادم]; **Tak-hash**[تكهش]; **Tarshayānah** [ترشيانه]; **Shūrat** [شورت]; **Taryānah** [تريانه]; **Nāshah** [ناشة]; **O Rawājānah** [رواجانة]; **Bāshah**

[باشه]; **Tarnawā** [ترنوا]; **Batayāmah** [بتيامه]; **Tashah** [تشه]; **Qawah** [قوه]; **O Hī** [هي], **Hī** [هي]; **Thahyān** [ثهيان]; **Thabyābam** [ثبيابم]; **Kajam** [كجم], **Kajam** [كجم], **Kajam** [كجم]; **Ḥakrī** [حكرى]; **Dahnah** [دهنة]; **by Dahnah** [دهنة]; **Barhayah** [برهية]; **Bārayah** [باريه]; **Ṭāshayā** [طاليا], **Ṭāshayā** [طاليا]; **Kashtah** [كشته], **Kashtah** [كشته]; **Ṭār** [طار]; **O Ṭār** [طار]; **O Thabthawā** [ثبثوا]; **Sharnathyā** [شرنثيا]; **Yabdī** [يبدي]; **Ḥandash** [حندش]; **Harehīm** [هرثيم]; **Marqashaymā** [مرقشيما]; **by Shafāhah** [شفاهه]; **Hawlayā** [هوليا]; **Mālayā** [ماليا]; **Hayah-yana** [هيهينا]; **'Arkar** [عركر]; **Kamānash** [كمانش]; **'Andarūsh** [عندروش]; **Qarqūsh** [قرقوش]; **'Armawāl** [عرموال], **'Armawāl** [عرموال]; **'Araj** [عرج]; **'Aw-'ayā** [عوعيا]; **Ḥafāj** [حفاج]; **'Anjal** [عنجل]; **Hayṭalaḥ** [هيطلح], **Hayqar** [هيقر]; **Hū** [هو], **Hū** [هو]; **Lord of Light Most High**. **Answer me**, **O Abū Ma'bad Zunbūr** [أبو معبد زنبور], **and**, **O Masṭā'ab** [مسطاعب], **and**, **O Abū Rūt** [أبو روت] **the Headsman**.

Know, **may the Lord guide you**, **that this seal is one of the hidden secrets and you can employ it for numerous kinds of illusions and wondrous works**, **such as**: **the manifestation of possessing jinn**; **evocation**; **reproval**; **subjugation**; **abduction**; **healing**; **enquiring about strange news throughout the regions of the earth**; **imprisonment**; **killing**; **assault**; **binding**; **binding tongues**; **the fulfillment of needs**; **harmony**; **love**; **arousal**; **causing illness**; **causing hemorrhage**; **incineration**; **transportation**; **hatred**; **demolishing inhabited areas**, **houses**, **mills**, **and buildings**; **whatever is required**, **with obedience**, **compliance**, **and quickness**; **and any real magic that is needed**, **be**

it great or small. It is a noble seal, comprising all that you desire.

The Binding, Crucifixion, And Interogation Of Jinn

If someone brings a possessed person to you, and a Wind from among the jinn is in him, write the following for him to make his possessing jinni manifest himself. When he manifests, order that the Wind be bound, saying, "Lafā [لفا], Lafā [لفا], Hay [هي], Hafyah [هفيه], Ay [اي], Hay [هي], Barhī [برهي]. Surrender by the right of Him who has dominion over ye, and by the right of 'Aqshayr Ṭahrash [عقشير طهرش]. Bind him, O Maymūn [ميمون]!"

If you wish the jinni to speak, then imprison him inside the body, saying, "I have imprisoned ye by Hanṭash [هنطش], Hanṭash [هنطش], Kāf Hā Yā 'Ayn Ṣād [كهيعص], and Ḥā Mīm 'Ayn Sīn Qāf [حم عسق]."

Asaph the son of Berechiah said: "If you wish to imprison a Wind inside a body, say these words: 'By Yadūm [يدوم], Nadah [نده], Anah [انه], Nayah [نيه], Kahar [كهر], Kahar [كهر], Qayūrash [قيورش], Sha'ash [شعش], Ṭarṭaqayūrash [طرطقيورش]. "Abiding therein for ages," confined, by the power of the Lord Most High. "And they could not stand, nor could they help themselves."' In addition, say these names over a thread from his yoke, wash it, tie its end, and place it around his neck or under his feet: 'Ahmī Hamī [اهمى همى]. And stop them, for they must be questioned.'"

Asaph the son of Berechiah said: If you wish to imprison a jinni inside a body and see him wail and weep, write these names on the floor with your finger:

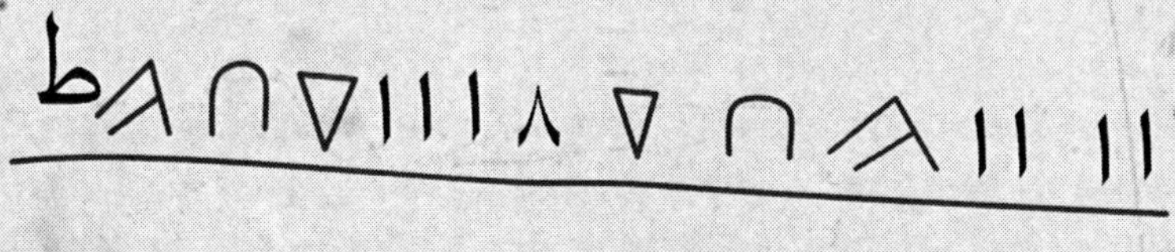

Likewise, if you write the following seal on the possessed person's forehead and tie his thumb, the jinni will not be able to leave until you free him. It is amazing, so do not underestimate it. It is a secret of secrets and a security from the jinn.

Asaph the son of Berechiah said, "The following is another interrogation. If you render a possessed person unconscious and wish to make the jinni speak, say these names in his ear:

Shalāṭī [شلاطي]; **Hāṭī** [هاطي]; **Haṭā'** [هطاء]; **Hūyal** [هويل]; **Sham'ayk** [شمعيك]; **Adonai**; **Yalāqam** [يلاقم]; **Mar'ūbā** [مرعوبا]; **the ill-tempered Tashyākan** [تشياكن]; **Qaṭī** [قطي], **Qaṭī** [قطي]. **Speak, O enemy of the Lord, by Him who will say unto Hell, "Are you full?" whereupon it will reply, "Is there more?" and by Him who said unto the heavens and the earth, "Come willingly or unwillingly," upon which they said, "We shall come willingly." Speak, O jinni, by the right of these names:**

Malaqna'aqsalaynaḥaj [ملقنعقسلينحج], **Kaya'safajfajar** [كيعسفجفجر], **Shamham** [شمهم], **Qawārash** [قوارش].' **Upon saying these names in his ear, he will speak and answer all your questions. It is wondrous and profound. Use it and safeguard it, for it is one the best secrets. If he does not speak, and you wish to crucify and hang him, then write "**اطط**" on his right hand, "**مطط**" on his left hand, "**طوا**"on his right leg, "**اقدم بشردل**"on his left leg, and "**قنا طويل اكرم مطط**" on his forehead. After that, say, 'By the right of these names, I entreat you to gather him in a single surprise attack. Hang him and raise him, by Him who did raise Enoch unto a lofty place. Sām Sām Azarīn Azarīn Hahar** [سام سام عزرين عزرين ههر], **Sām Sām Azarīn Azarīn Hahar** [سام سام عزرين عزرين ههر], **Sām Sām Azarīn Azarīn Hahar** [سام سام عزرين عزرين ههر], **Amlaykhā** [امليخا], **Rabb** [رب], **Jabbār** [جبار], **Fard** [فرد], **Ṣamad** [صمد], **'Adl** [عدل]. **I speak the truth**. **Rasūl** [رسول], **Dūsh** [دوش], **Lajīm** [لجيم]. **Hang him, by Him who says unto a thing "Be!" whereupon it is, O company of Aides**! **Make him speak, O Mahāayā'īl** [مهصيائيل]! **Rebuke him, O Dardā'īl** [دردائيل]. **Burn him, O Ṭalahkafā'īl** [طلهكفائيل], **by Shayhakah** [شيهكة], **Haylah** [هيلة], **Hayah** [هيه], **Hayd** [هيد], **Sharūkh** [شروخ], **Barshūkh** [برشوخ]. **Hang him and make him speak, by the right of the Ahayṭalūsh** [اهيطلوش] **Most Great. Break him into pieces, by the right of Him who raised Elias unto a high place.**'

The Employments Of Hamanah [حامنه], And A Discussion Of His Seal

Asaph the son of Berechiah, the son of Shemuel, the son of Shimea, said, "If you desire fast service, make use of the service of Ḥāmanah [حامنه]. He is an Aide of potent obedience and quick compliance. He has been tested and found to be the quickest there is in this science. He has a number of rebel jinn and Ruhaniyyah only the Lord, Mighty and Majestic, can enumerate. It is a secret of secrets."

For his seal, write these noble names upon jet in silver:

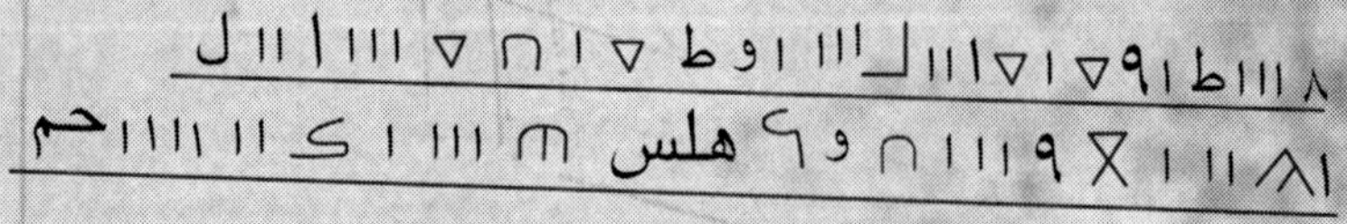

Asaph the son of Berechiah said: "Following are some of the specialties of Ḥāmanah's [حامنه] wonders:

If you wish to visit a possessed person but fear that he will hold out against you, then say these names over black pebbles and write them thereon as well. Then enter his room and strike the floor with the pebbles and this will make his possessing jinni manifest in the most violent manner. If he does not resist you, write the names on his palm, say them over the pebbles, and strike the floor therewith and this will make his possessing jinni manifest. The names are as follows: 'Lak-hakash [لكهكش], **Namūh** [نموه], **Ḥāmanah** [حامنه], **Ṣahaṭlī** [صهطلى], **Ḥasmī** [حسمي], **Maha'aynawā** [مهعينوا], **Hūrash** [هورش], **Hanah** [هنه], **Ḥāmanah** [حامنه], **Shafāhah** [شفاهة]."

Asaph said, "If you fear that one of the healers or scholars will veil you when you visit a possessed person, say the following words and then command as you wish and it will make his possessing jinni manifest. These are the words: Kaykahatlayārash [كيكهتليارش], **Mahīṭ** [مهيط], **Hūkash** [هوكش], **Qarqar** [قرقر], **Kasar** [كسر], **Kasar** [كسر], **Ahī** [اهي], **Ṭahkasar** [طهكسر], **Namwā** [نموا], **Ḥāmanah** [حامنه], **Shafāhah** [شفاهة]."

Asaph said, "If you have rendered the possessed person unconscious and wish to imprison the jinni inside the body, then write صابور صابور شيتا شيتا **between the person's eyes and** عكشيا عكشيا عطشيا و قيل اقعدوا مع القاعدين **on his legs and charge Ḥāmanah** [حامنه]."

Asaph said, "If you visit a possessed person and with you is a group of scholars, and you wish to shield the possessing jinni from them, so that they will be unable to make him manifest or evoke, write the following words on either a palm leaf, silk hem, or knife, and recite them and you will see a wonder. The words are as follows: Ṣahkatī [صهكتى], Hawrad [هورد], Hawrad [هورد], Ṭayhatamharash [طيهتمهرش], Harash [هرش], Ahrash [اهرش], Maylah [ميله], Harash [هرش], Ṭayharash [طيهرش], Aktahī [اكتهي], Aktahī [اكتهي], Dahkatī [دهكتي]. 'You see them looking at you, but they see not.' And if you wish to undo it, wash it in water and it will go away."

Asaph said, "If you wish to have any of the celestial or terrestrial Ruhaniyyah brought to you quicker than the flash of lightning, say the following seven names, which are a secret of the angel Mīṭaṭrūn [ميططرون]: Arkūsh [اركوش], Kanhūsh [كنهوش], Kalhūsh [كلهوش], Kanhūsh [كنهوش], Armāsh [ارماش], Kanhūsh [كنهوش], Almashtarā [المشترا], Qāmūsh [قاموش]. Make haste to bring me King N, king of the jinn."

Asaph said, "If someone is withholding a possessing jinni from among the major or minor spirits, or one of the kings, whether celestial or terrestrial, from you, then both he and the one witholding him will be brought quicker than the flash of lightning. Say the following names, which are the names by which the Lord created the angels who are in charge of the jinn's fore-

locks. Therefore, say it only on important occassions. You say: 'By the right of Saṭfaymashā [سطفيمشا], **Kaklī** [ككلي], **Darash** [درش], **Hūmayash** [هوميش], **Yā Thāmanat** [يا ثامنت], **Halā** [هلا], **Hathlātah** [هثلاته], **Hat-hatat** [هتهتت], **Hashhashah** [هشهشة], **Hashhashah** [هشهشة], **Hawīl** [هويل], **Hawīl** [هويل], **Hatāyīl** [هتاييل], **Hatāyīl** [هتاييل], **Ḥamash** [حمش], **Nūsh** [نوش], **Hashūsh** [هشوش], **Mūrash** [مورش]. **O angels of my Lord, bring me N and whoever is withholding him.' Thereupon they will bring him to you quicker than the flash of lightning, without effort. If you wish, you may say, 'I summon you, O company of pure spirits from among those obedient to God, Lord of the Worlds, who has the jinn and devils by the forelocks, by that which Solomon the son of David said; by God, my Lord and your Lord, Creator of all things, God of all things, who has power over all things—wherever ye may be in the kingdom of the Lord, Mighty and Majestic—by the right of Shaṭāṭ** [شطاط], **Ṭāṭ** [طاط], **Nūh** [نوه], **Nūh** [نوه], **Ah** [اه], **Ah** [اه], **Shawāh** [شواة], **Shawāh** [شواة], **Anhā** [انها], **Anhā** [انها], **Shamakh** [شمخ], **Shamakh** [شمخ], **Asha'āl** [عشعال], **Asha'āl** [عشعال], **Ghashayāl** [غشيال], **Maznayāsh** [مزنياش], **Maznayāsh** [مزنياش], **Ṣabūsh** [صبوش], **Būsh** [بوش], **Markayūsh** [مركيوش], **Mayāsh** [مياش], **Nūsh** [نوش], **Ah** [اه], **Hawāh** [هواه], **Hū** [هو], **the Lord of Light Most High who speaks with infinite speech, Shamūs** [شموس], **Habūṭ** [هبوط], **Habūṭ** [هبوط], **Ah** [اه], **Hawāh** [هواه], **Kaykanāsh** [كيكناش], **Kaykanāsh** [كيكناش], **Marnayāsh** [مرنياش], **Marnayāsh** [مرنياش], **Mayūsh** [ميوش]. **I am the Divine, who alone possesses Oneness.**

Līkhā [ليخا]. Līkhā [ليخا]. Descend ye upon this rebel from among the Ruhaniyyah (here you state his name, be he a king or otherwise, or from a tribe or otherwise, whether small or great).'"

Asaph also said, "If you wish to imprison one of the Kings or spirits, even if he is in the east and you are in the west, say these names and state his name and he will be imprisoned and remain so until you free him. If someone summons you to a possessed person and you say them before reaching him, it will facilitate his matter for you, with effort on your part. Likewise, if you enter a possessed person's room and one of the scholars claiming knowledge about the spiritual sciences is with you, and you speak these names, it will restrain and bind them in their homes, and you shall command as you are commanded. Do likewise if you wish to bind their leader and their kings. The names are as follows: 'Ūratayāsh [مورتياش], Anqāṭarūnīsh [انقاطرونيش], Damīsh [دميش], Mankafash [منكفش], Alwāhaynūsh [الواهينوش], Rūmashāsh [رومشاش], Ṭarnayūsh [طرنيوش], Ṣahyarūsh [صهيروش]. Turn ye them upside down and bind them, by the strength and power of the Creator. Mahūbayāh [مهوبياه]."

Asaph said, "If you wish them to be annihilated altogether, indiscriminately, then say the Names of Annihilation, as follows: Aqwā [اقوا], Aynūf [اينوف], Kahfūf [كهفوف], Rūhāwuf [وروهاوف], Ramūm [رموم], Rayāq [رياق], Sharūf [شروف], Hārūf [هاروف]. Seize them and destroy them, O Mīṭaṭrūn

[ميططرون], **quickly! And witness the wonder.”**

Asaph related the following from Solomon the son of David: “If you enter a sitting and fear that one of the celestial or terrestrial Kings will block you, say these words before entering the house and before summoning your aides: Karnafīsh [كرنفيش], **Marwādīsh** [مرواديش], **Kawānaqūsh** [كوانقوش], **Marhūbasāsh** [مرهوبساش], **Marhūbasāsh** [مرهوبساش], **Sharūmīsh** [شروميش], **Bikahyārish** [بكهيارش], **Nadrash** [ندرش], **Rabb, Rabb. ‘He does not fear being overtaken, nor is he afraid.’ ‘I have protected my soul and body with God Most Great. O angels of my Lord!’ Then order your aides to cling to you under your clothes and not harm you or do anything to your body, and recite these names: ‘Ahwarmayāṭ** [اهورمياط], **Hūnāraṭ** [هونارط], **Hashlū** [هشلو], **Abhataṭ** [ابهتط], **Karmahayūṭ** [كرمهيوط], **Lāhūr** [لاهور], **Yā Nūṭ** [يا نوط], **Shalkarū** [شلكرو], **Mayṭ** [ميط], **Rathyāwuṭ** [رثياوط], **Tahwāyaṭ** [تهوايط], **Jibrīl** [جبريل], **Mīkā'īl** [ميكائيل]. **Come to me, O angels of my Lord. Come ye quick as the flash of lightning, and aid me with your lights from afar lest harm befall my aides. When you enter the assembly and angels are with you, say these names: Tūmar** [تومر], **Hūsh** [هوش], **Handūsh** [هندوش], **Lahyārash** [لهيارش], **Darakfayāsh** [دركفياش], **Arnāwush** [ارناوش], **Darnūsh** [درنوش], **Ahdaqaysh** [اهدقيش].”

“If you do not wish one of their aides to enter a house or a place in which you will be, say the following words: Hawā [هوا], **Shalman** [شلمن], **O**

Mahūk [مهوك], Fahmūk [فهموك], Darhamūk [درهموك], Anqād [انقاد], Wamāk [وماك], Sahalūk [سهلوك], Afahūlā [افهولا], Mayāk [مياك], Hālūk [هالوك]. Then order your aides to come out from under your clothes, and do whatever you wish, and your command will be obeyed without effort on your part. When you complete the operation, secure yourself and your aides with the following names, which are an amulet of encompassing light, and which the angels of Lot said, whereupon the Lord Most High veiled them from his people, so they could see neither Lot nor the angels, as the names veiled from them. You say: Mahamyashhashūh [مهميشهشوه], Lahyāmah [لهيامه], Hūmayah [هوميه], Wahashūmah [وهشومه], Fahū [فهو], Nashalūmah [نشلومه], Anūdamah [انودمه], Daṭyāmah [دطيامه]. 'We are messengers of thy Lord. They will not reach thee.' I have protected myself, my wealth, and my son with the Divine, al-'Aẓīm [العظيم], al-Ṣamad [صمد], ar-Rafī' [الرفيع], al-Qāhir [القاهر], al-Badī' [البديع], al-Qawiyy [القوي], al-Manī' [المنيع], the Almighty who has no end, the Overpowering and Glorious who cannot be harmed. Blessed is God, our Lord, the Owner of Majesty and Generosity."

Commentary on the Pentacle

This is the pentacle that Solomon the son of David possessed, the great Altar concerning which he made a pact with the spirits, and upon which Jibrīl [جبريل], Mīkā'īl [ميكائيل], Isrāfīl [إسرافيل], and 'Azrā'īl [عزرائيل] sat, on the day he made a pact with the spirits.

Asaph the son of Berechiah said, "These names were revealed to Solomon the son of David in the Divine language and are beyond the comprehension of the priests from among the jinn and humankind. They charge the jinn with a great task. Whenever Solomon wished to kill an oppressive ifreet, he would unfold them, whereupon all the people, jinn and birds around him would tremble. The spiritual angels will hasten to them from your right and left. Take them out only out of necessity, and do not hasten to use them or else you will harm yourself. Twelve angels serve them. They are the ones that Ibn Ba'ura al-Farisi said were on the banner of Solomon the son of David; when the wind would subside, he would unfold it and the wind would blow anywhere he wished."

Asaph the son of Berechiah said, "If you wish to construct it, write the names on a piece of red or white silk cloth, attach this to a branch of a boxthorn, a pomegranate, or a quince, and then unfold it and you will see wonders. If you undertake this at night, light seven candles under it, pitch seven tents over them, and attach a banner identical to the main banner to each one. If it is done during the day, then put it somewhere secluded from others, and do not light anything. Moreoever, it should be remote from any habitation, somewhere clean and pure. Your clothes should be clean as well. When you finish constructing it, you will have a banner raised upon four pillars above the ground before you. If a powerful possessing jinni defies you, if a discord arises between you and one of the Spiritual Kings, if one of the Kings forms a party against you and you fear for yourself, if armies of jinn join forces against you, if a sage from among the scholars charges spirits to harm you, if you want something important from a king of the jinn or human race, such as the fulfullment of lofty needs, the freeing of a prisoner sentenced to death, or the demotion of a particular individual, or if someone tyrannizes his kingdom, distance yourself from any habitation, and do not be frightened. Cast a mandal around yourself and on a mirror, lay the mirror before you, and summon the celestial Ruhaniyyah in charge of all the planets. Alternatively, you can write an amulet and banishments for yourself on some saucers, wash them off with water, and sprinkle it on the floor until it becomes wet.

You do this for fear of the Diver Jinn. In addition, write an amulet for yourself on your right side, on your left side, on your head, and below you. When they come, ask your need of them and the Divine will fulfill it for you.

"If you wish that a transgressive ifreet from among the kings be killed, carry out your command concerning him, and observe piety. Stay away from filth. Keep to cleanliness, humility and forbearance. Beware of ostentation, as it is a means of stumbling. Thank the Lord Most High for what He has given you, as it is a means of increase. If you wish to have information of news from the east to the west, ask the Traversers in the regions of the earth and they will inform you thereof. If you want them to transport you over the distance of a year's journey in a single instant, make a carpet with them, place it under you, and say the names of the Ruhaniyyah. If you wish to assist the citizens of your country against an enemy they are powerless to resist, recite the names and empower whomever you wish over him. If you want to make a pact wth any of the kings of the jinn, then summon him and say: Shāh [شاه], Shāh [شاه], Ash [اش], Ash [اش], Layāl [ليال], Layāl [ليال], Ḥālif [حالف], Ḥālif [حالف]. And when thy Lord took their descendants out from the loins of the children of Adam and made them testify about themselves, saying, "Am I not your Lord? They said, Yes. We bear witness." If he complies, covenant with him; otherwise recite the names written on the center of the pentacle and blow on him and he will burn. I have

given a summary for fear of lengthiness (the names have a thousand uses). They are the Supreme Obedience that Solomon the son of David used, and which he used to take with himself from country to country. You can use them to subordinate all the inhabitants of the Earth. Safeguard what has come to you, O scholar, and do not reveal it to an ignoramus, for he will use it for something that God Most High does not approve of. Safeguard them, just as I have told you.

"If you wish to kill a king, draw the pentacle on a clean piece of parchment and draw a figure in the center of it. Then write the first line—the one in the uppermost part of the center of the circle—on its neck, the right line, to the right of it, the left line, to the left of it, and the two names that are in the lowermost part of the center of the circle, on the center of it, and command as you wish. When you wish to kill him, draw a figure of him, say his name, and insert a knife into any name or letter in the figure you wish and he will be killed. If you wish to beat him, then beat the figure with a rope fixed to a pomegranate branch.

"These are the names of the ifreets who serve the pentacle: al-Madhhab [المذهب], Yazīd ibn al-Ḥakīm [يزيد بن الحكيم], 'Umar ibn Jābir [عمر بن جابر], Fayqaṭūsh [فيقطوش], Marqīl [مرقيل], Abū Ma'shar [أبو معشر], Abū al-Rahab [أبو الرهب], Abū al-Ḥakam [أبو الحكم], 'Abd al-Raḥmān al-Mukhṭib [عبد الرحمن المخطب], al-Humayl [الهميل] the Invisible Flyer, Abu al-Hawl [أبو الهول], 'Āsif al-Riyāḥ [عاصف الرياح], Ṣakhr [صخر], Shamardal the Flyer [شمردل], Khandash [خندش], Naykal [نيكل], Shamhūrash [شمهورش], Burqān [برقان], Zawba'ah [زوبعة], Maymūn as-Saḥābiyy [ميمون الصحابي], Maymūn al-Ghamāmiyy [ميمون الغمامي], Maymūn al-Kanāwī [ميمون الكناوي], Samlaq the Flyer [سملق], and al-'Amlāq [العملاق]. They are the servants of the pentacle; they are twenty-four ifreets.

The following are the four ifreets in charge of the four corners of the carpet of Solomon the son of David: Damrayāṭ the Ifreet [دمرياط], **Shūghāl** [شوغال], **Hadlabāj** [هدلباج], **and Ṣay'atī** [صيعتى]. **This their secret and their subjugation:**

Say: Shahashlaṭūsh [شهشلطوش], **Shaṭīṭ** [شطيط], **Ṭafakūsh** [طفكوش], **Ḥajaj** [حجج], **Kashkash** [كشكش], **Lay'atūsh** [ليعتوش], **Shahash** [شهش], **Laṭūsh** [لطوش]. **Obey your Creator, O company of ifreets!**

"Following is a conjuration to the Ruhaniyyah in charge of the carpet. It is called 'the Helpful Conjuration.' For several hours of the daytime, the angels, the jinn of the sky, the airy jinn, the watery jinn, the jinn of the trees, the earthy jinn, the fiery jinn, the Tempters, and the Snatchers in charge of the children of Adam gather round it. It consists of eighty words. It is the Spiritual Conjuration and has three hundred uses. Therein are the names written in the center of the Sun, the three names written in the center of the Moon, the names written in the center of Mars, the names written in the center of Mercury, the names written in the center of Jupiter, the names written in the center of Saturn, the seven names by which the Lord created humankind, the seven names by which God created the angels who are in charge of the trees and plants, five names that magicians from among the jinn and of the land of Babel would use, and the seven names written in the center of the Talisman. Among them is also the Expediting Name, which you write on a citron leaf, wash off with rose

water and honey from an unfumigated comb, and give to drink to whomever you wish to be inflamed with your love. Additionally, if you write it on a clean parchment with the blood of a martin and rub it on the head of a beast, it will obey you. You can do the same to a human. It has countless uses."

The Syriac Conjuration

After the first spiritual glorification, say: Arī [ارى], **Arī** [ارى], **Kafaytā** [كفيتا], **Kafaytā** [كفيتا], **Shalshahīsh** [شلشهيش], **Shalshahīsh** [شلشهيش], **Malshahīsh** [ملشهيش], **Malshahīsh** [ملشهيش], **Ahyalīl** [اهيليل], **Ahyalīl** [اهيليل], **Haybūl** [هيبول], **Haybūl** [هيبول], **Maltīt** [ملتيت], **Maltīt** [ملتيت], **Kalkayām** [كلكيام], **Kalkayām** [كلكيام], **Ahyal** [اهيل], **Ahyal** [اهيل], **Kalkathūm** [كلكثوم], **Kalkathūm** [كلكثوم], **Arayrī** [اريرى], **Arayrī** [اريرى]. **Answer me, answer me, Akyāhūm** [اكياهوم], **Akyāhūm** [اكياهوم], **Kalkayā'īl** [كلكيائيل], **Kalkayā'īl** [كلكيائيل], **by Damlākh** [دملاخ], **Barākh** [براخ], **Barākh** [براخ], **Hayṭayā'īl** [هيطيائيل], **Hayṭayā'īl** [هيطيائيل], **Arbāb** [ارباب], **Yā Rabb** [يا رب], **Haytanākh** [هيتناخ], **Haytanākh** [هيتناخ], **Maltayāhūkh** [ملتياهوخ], **Maltayāhūkh**

[ملتياهوخ], **Aqṭalah** [اقطله], **‘Ayṭalah** [عيطله], **Ajrayā’īl** [اجرائيل], **Ṭaylahūb** [طيلهوب], **Ṭaylahūb** [طيلهوب], **Ṭaylaṭūb** [طيلطوب], **Ṭaylaṭūb** [طيلطوب], **Haybawuṭ** [هيباوط], **Haybawuṭ** [هيباوط], **Kaylayā’īl** [كيليائيل], **Kaylayā’īl** [كيليائيل], **Kalmayā’īl** [كلميائيل], **Kalmayā’īl** [كلميائيل], **Damlākh** [دملاخ], **Barākh** [براخ], **Barākh** [براخ], **Jawlā** [جولا], **Jawlā** [جولا], **Haylā** [هيلا], **Haylā** [هيلا], **Shamlā** [شملا], **Shamlā** [شملا], **Staṭāf** [ستطاف], **Staṭāf** [ستطاف], **Ṣafīf** [صفيف], **Ṣafīf** [صفيف], **Maṭūf** [مطوف], **Maṭūf** [مطوف], **Khaṭāf** [خطاف], **Khaṭāf** [خطاف], **Ṭāyif** [طايف], **Ṭāyif** [طايف], **Sha‘dayāsh** [شعدياش], **Shaqdayāsh** [شقدياش], **Wardayāsh** [وردياش], **Shara‘ūn** [شرعون], **Shara‘ūn** [شرعون], **Jawḥashām** [جوحشام], **Jawḥashām** [جوحشام], **Maylā** [ميلا], **Maylā** [ميلا], **Salṭālīn** [سلطالين], **Saṭālīn** [سطالين], **Mahlawān** [مهلوان], **Mahlawān** [مهلوان], **Khabyaṭānā** [خبيطانا], **Abarūsh** [ابروش], **Jarūsh** [جروش], **Kalūsh** [كلوش], **Kalūsh** [كلوش], **Ṭaqshar** [طقشر], **Ṭaqshar** [طقشر], **Shalāmīn** [شلامين], **Raṭqash** [رطقش], **Raṭqash** [رطقش], **Shalīm** [شليم], **Shalīm** [شليم], **Kashāshūn** [كشاشون], **Kabshāshūn** [كبشاشون], **Yabtalah** [يبتلة], **Haytalah** [هيتلة], **Haytalūm** [هيتلوم], **Haytalūm** [هيتلوم], **Maltāhā** [ملتاها], **Maltāhā** [ملتاها], **Hayāl** [هيال], **Hayāl** [هيال], **Han** [هن], **Han** [هن], **Khaf** [خف], **Khaf** [خف], **Shadah** [شده], **Shadah** [شده], **Ḍayf** [ضيف], **Ḍayf** [ضيف], **Dalkham** [دلخم], **Dalkham** [دلخم], **Kashkam** [كشكم], **Kashkam** [كشكم], **Barūqā** [بروقا], **Barūqā** [بروقا], **Kashtah** [كشته], **Kashtah** [كشته], **Kashlā** [كشلا], **Kashlā** [كشلا], **Kashnadā** [كشندا], **Kashnadā** [كشندا], **‘Aqtaham** [عقتهم], **‘Aqtaham** [عقتهم], **Yūqatam** [يوقتم], **Yūqatam** [يوقتم], **Taqūfah** [تقوفه],

Taqūfah [تقوفه], **Dareayāwub** [درتياوب], **Dareayāwub** [درتياوب].

This is the secret Expediting Name, **of which the masters make mention**: **Yūh**, **Yūh**, **by Hayhalayūh** [هيهليوه], **Hayhalayūh** [هيهليوه]; **Alārakyāẓ** [الاركياظ], **Alārakyāẓ** [الاركياظ]; **Haybūr** [هيبور], **Haybūr** [هيبور]; **Kasaryāwub** [كسرياوب], **Kasaryāwub** [كسرياوب]; **'Alshaqūm** [علشقوم], **'Alshaqūm** [علشقوم]; **'Alshāqash** [علشاقش] **'Alshāqash** [علشاقش]; **Mahrāqash** [مهراقش], **Mahrāqash** [مهراقش]; **Aqshāmaqash** [اقشامقش]; **'Aqash** [عقش]; **Ṭahshīz** [طهشيز]; **Ehieh Asher Ehieh**; **Quddūs** [قدوس]; **Quddūs** [قدوس];**Lord of the angels and the Spirit**; **Ahyatān** [اهيتان], **Rakshān** [ركشان]; **Kashlakh** [كشلخ]; **Qashalmaqash** [قشلمقش]; **Qashalmaqash** [قشلمقش]; **Rāsh** [راش]; **Ayshāyaqash** [ايشايقش]; **Tadar** [تدر]; **Tayār** [تيار], **Tayār** [تيار]; **Kaytāl** [كيتال]; **Ḥayāhūm** [حياهوم]; **Bayāṣūm** [بياصوم]; **'Alyāḥam** [علياحم]; **Wabahāyam** [وبهايم]; **Ṭalṭayākh** [طلطياخ]; **Aḥyākam** [احياكم]; **Rafyādīm** [رفياديم]; **'Ashyāram** [عشيارم]; **Jaryākam** [جرياكم]; **Jabarūt** [جبروت], **Jabarūt** [جبروت]; **'Alyāham** [علياهم], **'Alyāham** [علياهم]; **Ḥajbāwut** [حجباوت]; **Warawāyab** [وروايب]; **Sharyā** [شريا]; **'Awalīn** [عولين] **'Awalīn** [عولين]; **Kalkalahūj** [كلكلهوج], **Kalkalahūj** [كلكلهوج]; **Jarkhayāl** [جرخيال] **Jarkhayāl** [جرخيال]; **Yakṭashah** [يكطشه]; **Yashṭamah** [يشطمه]; **'Anjahaf** [عنجهف]; **Ṣanah** [صنه], **Ṣanah** [صنه]; **A'aḥakān** [ععحكان]; **Fūkh** [فوخ]; **Ka'aydākh** [كعيداخ]; **'Asmaylāh** [عسميلاه]; **Ah** [اه], **Ah** [اه], **Ah** [اه]; **El**, **El**; **Quddūs** [قدوس] **Quddūs** [قدوس];

Lord of the angels and the Spirit; **Laṭashmah** [لطشمه]; **Hah** [هه]; **El**; **Quddūs** [قدوس], **who is capable of whatsoever He wills**; **Ṣaylayākhūt** [صيلياخوت]; **Arbāhūṭ** [ارباهوط]; **Yā Baṭarhaytā** [بطرهيتا]; **Yā Lamahaytā** [لمهيتا]; **Aḥbāyashā** [احبايشا]; **Haytalāmatā** [هيتلامتا]; **Matūbā** [متوبا]; **'Alkamashā** [علكمشا]; **Falmalhayā** [فلملهيا]; **Yaṭīkh** [يطيخ]; **Yaṭam** [يطم]; **Ṭaythā** [طيثا]; **Ḥamā** [حما]; **Ḥamaythā** [حميثا]; **Ḥathaythā** [حثيثا]; **El Shaddi**; **El**; **Khūsh** [خوش]; **Shandalūn** [شندلون], **Shandalūn** [شندلون]; **Yā Handawān** [يا هندوان]; **Yā Malīkhā** [يامليخا]; **Azrayā** [ازريا], **Azrayā** [ازريا]; **Subbūḥ** [سبوح], **Subbūḥ** [سبوح], **Quddūs** [قدوس], **Quddūs** [قدوس], **Lord of the angels and the Spirit**; **Aldākh** [الداخ], **Danshalākh** [دنشلاخ]; **Wanāshākh** [وناشاخ]; **Mar'āwī** [مرعاوي]; **Maṣrāyīm** [مصرابيم]; **Tzabaoth**; **'Abadūyā** [عبدويا]; **Alhaybā** [الهيبا]; **Aylahā** [ايلها], **God of the angels and the Spirit**; **Yāh** [ياه]; **Yah** [يه], **Yah** [يه],**Yah** [يه], **Yah** [يه]; **Quddūs** [قدوس], **Quddūs** [قدوس]; **Asalbawā** [اسلبوا]; **Ṭawāshah** [طواشه]; **Bakhyā** [بخيا]; **Balyā** [بليا]; **Qalyā** [قليا]; **Mashdīd** [مشديد]; **Falbāwum** [فلباوم]; **Daḥūt** [دحوت]; **Akhwā** [اخوا] [**x**2]; **Lamyāh** [لمياه]; **Lā** [لا]; **Ḥarāj** [حراج]; **Rawad** [رود]; **Zayd** [زيد]; **Adam** [ادم]; **Dayūsh** [ديوش]; **Qalnaṣūdam** [قلنصودم]; **Yashāṭūr** [يشاطور] [**x**2]; **Falqahaṣūdam** [فلقهصودم]; **Arfāf** [ارفاف]; **Armayārūsh** [ارمياروش]; **Kashrayāwub** [كشرياوب]; **Damareīthā** [دمرتيثا]; **Wamareayā** [ومرتيا]; **Artayād** [ارتياد]; **Yālīn** [يالين]; **Mayārah** [مياره]; **Damarkūsh** [دمركوش]; **Dayāṭūr** [دياطور]; **Laḥtatar** [لحتتر]; **Amīn** [امين]; **Dād** [داد]; **Madād** [مداد]; **Yūyah** [يويه]; **Qalayṭāyūh** [قليطانوه]; **Yūthar** [يوثر]; **Fūthar** [فوثر]; **Adād** [اداد]; **Ad-**

mād [ادماد]. I conjure you, O company of jinn, devils, ifreets, giants, ghouls, tempters, and Danāhishah [دناهشة], and you, O Burqān [برقان]; and by the right of the names of your Lord which are in this conjuration, and their sanctity unto you, to come from where ye are, by these words, and (here you state your need). Whosoever of you disobeys this has disbelieved, disobeyed, and rebelled.

The Burning Names

They are the names with which you torture the spirits. If a Wind disobeys you, write these names on a piece of paper and beat it with a pomegranate branch. They are the following names:

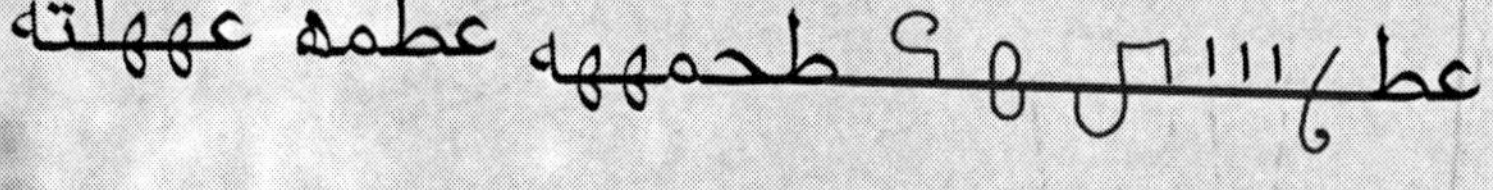

Possession

This is for all the tribes of the jinn. You write it on the possessed person's palm and recite it. It has powerful ifreets. It is as follows: "Aṭlat [اطلت], **Qūsh** [قوش], **Aṭaysha'ūsh** [اطيشعوش], **Qūrūsh** [قوروش], **'Akaykayūsh** [عكيكيوش], **Ṭabaykar** [طبيكر], **'Akaykawā** [عكيكوا], **Harmayā** [حرميا], **Wamaryā** [ومريا], **Wakhathaythā** [وخثيثا], **Shahūsh** [شهوش], **Shatwāh** [شتواه], **Nashūh** [نشوه].

Extracted Secrets Consisting of Names

First Secret: For 'Umar ibn Jābir [عمر بن جابر]. **You say: You are my Lord, Tharam** [ثرم], **Hasham** [هشم], **Mā Tharmān Ḥayhā** [ما ثرمان حيها],

Mā Tharmān Ba'dī [ما ثرمان بعدي], **Mā Tharmān Radad Wadad** [ما ثرمان ردد ودد], **Mā Tharmān** [ما ثرمان]. **Answer**, **O 'Umar ibn Jābir** [عمر بن جابر], **and obey my command**, **by the right of these names**.

Second Secret: **For Mahāqīl** [مهاقيل]. **You say these names**: **Yā Wanwā** [يا ونوا], **Yā Baryā** [بريا], **Atā** [اتا], **Rabwāl** [ربوال], **Ash** [اش], **Shāshā** [شاشا], **Ayan** [اين], **Kālish** [كالش], **Maḥma'ar** [محمعر], **Yābahā** [يابها], **Kālā** [كالا], **Tashrīn** [تشرين], **Ṭahaykh** [طهيخ], **Haykh** [هيخ], **Aza'at** [ازعت], **Aza'at** [ازعت]. **Obey my command**, **O Mahāqīl** [مهاقيل], **by the right of these names**.

Third Secret: **For Faqṭash** [فقطش]. **You say**: **Abrayā** [ابريا], **Baṭayr** [بطير], **Asyār** [اسيار], **Ashāqūr** [اشاقور], **Ashqār** [اشقار], **Aqfad** [اقفد], **Dayā** [ديا], **Walam** [ولم], **Dasharūkh** [دشروخ], **Alham** [الهم], **Aywālah** [ايواله], **Alam** [الم], **Alūyan** [الوين], **'Amā** [عما], **Aqwāṭīr** [اقواطير]. **And they imagine kinship between Him and the jinn**, **whereas thejinn know well that they will be brought**. **Answer**, **O sincere servants of the Lord**!

Fourth Secret: **For Shajaljalash** [شجلجلش], **in Indian. You say**: **Awam** [اوم], **Nawī** [نوي], **Namū** [نمو], **Bahkaythawā** [بهاكيثوا], **Shahramat** [شهرمت], **Shadhab** [شدهب], **Ḥāthayth** [حاثيث], **Shalā** [شلا], **Hakshah** [هكشه], **Laynawā** [لينوا], **Radī** [ردي], **Mayah** [ميه], **Hayah** [هيه], **Thaynah** [ثينه], **Anshayah** [انشيه], **Ayshatah** [ايشته], **Mandalah** [مندله], **Jahah** [جهه], **Jahah** [جهه], **Shafah** [شفه], **Dāqād** [داقاد], **Yadwī** [يدوي], **Baydā**

[بيدا], **Shafāhah** [شفاهة]. **Make haste, O Shajaljalash** [شجلجلش], **and obey my command, by the right of these names.**"

Fifth Secret: For Malik ibn 'Uryah [مالك بن عرية], **in Indian. You say: By Hak'aj** [هكعج], **Layḥajlakh** [ليحجلخ], **Shaqār** [شقر], **Taltahīkh** [تلتهيخ], **Tak-hashīkh** [تكهشيخ], **Laylakh** [ليلخ], **Lakh** [لخ], **Taykah** [تيكه], **Lay-jahā** [ليجها], **Raqash** [رقش], **Hakmash** [هكمش], **Ḥashrā** [حشرا], **Yazṭah** [يزطه], **Yarhashān** [يرهشان], **Raqah** [رقه], **Hakaylaḥashū** [هكيلحشو], **Kakash** [ككش], **Faylabarā** [فيلبرا], **Ayṭaṭar** [ايططر], **Ṭūrash** [طورش]. **Hasten, O Mālik ibn 'Uryah** [مالك بن عرية], **and obey my command, by the right of these names.**

Sixth Secret: For 'Āmūdayā [عاموديا], **in Indian. You say: Namū** [نمو], **Shaydīkh** [شيديخ], **Ḥāmandī** [حامندي], **Ḥāmandī** [حامندي], **Yūrashīr** [يورشير], **Kayāl** [كيال], **Mālah** [ماله], **Ay** [اى], **Samī** [سمى], **Dhī** [ذي], **Sam** [سم], **Mahyam** [مهيم], **Shām** [شام], **Samārahūl** [سمارهول], **Marhūb** [مرهوب], **Aykal** [ايكل], **Yūyūlash** [يويولش], **Mānash** [مانش], **Shūn** [شون], **Shūrī** [شوري], **Yūmāhī** [يوماهي], **Yarāhā** [يراها], **Barmāhī** [برماهي], **Wamāhī** [وماهي], **Laṭrah** [لطره], **Laṭrah** [لطره], **Hayā** [هيا], **Hayā** [هيا], **Shāhā** [شاها], **Ṭahmayah** [طهميه], **Lahmayah** [لهميه], **Shūrā** [شورا], **Shūt** [شوت], **Taṭlī** [تطلي], **Shūrā** [شورا], **Yakwī** [يكوي], **Kashtah** [كشته], **Ay** [اي], **Nāy** [ناي], **Shaqlafah** [شقلفه]. **Hurry, O 'Āmūdayā** [عاموديا], **King of the Generation, the Smoke, by the right of these names.**

Seventh Secret: **For Zunbūr** [زنبور]. **You say**: **Ḥoh** [حوه], **Ḥoh** [حوه], **Adam** [ادم], **Takmahash** [تكمهش], **Qareayānah** [قرتيانه], **Shawqar** [شوقر], **Ghānah** [غانة], **Rath** [رث], **Tharmānah** [ثرمانه], **Yāshah** [ياشه], **Yā Rawājāyah** [يا رواجايه], **Yā Shah** [يا شه], **Yadlawā** [يدلوا], **Baqayāmah** [بقيامه], **Thathah** [ثته], **Qawah** [قوه], **Yā Ḥayy** [يا حي], **Tāhī** [تاهى], **Tayshāl** [تيشال], **Yathnāyam** [يثنايم], **Kajam** [كجم], **Kajam** [كجم], **Ḥakrī** [حكري], **Badhayah** [بدهية], **Tharhayah** [ثرهية], **Barhayah** [برهية], **Bādayah** [بادية], **Ṭāthayā** [طاثيا], **Kashtah** [كشته], **Kashtah** [كشته], **Ṭārayā** [طاريا], **Ṭārayā** [طاريا], **Taqyawā** [تقيوا], **Shar** [شر], **Laythayātayad** [ليثياتيد], **Anshadī** [انشدي], **Jandī** [جندي], **Hawsham** [هوشم], **Marqash** [مرقش], **Ashfāhah** [اشفاهة]. **Haste**, **O Zunbūr** [زنبور] **and Mashṭā'ib** [مشطاعب], **and obey my command**."

Eighth Secret: **For Maymūn** [ميمون] **and Bilāl** [بلال], **in Indian. Say**: **Shak-khaklāyāhīsh** [شكخكلياهيش], **Warajūr** [ورجور], **Ta'shī** [تعشى], **Qashkandūrash** [قشكندورش], **Kayūd** [كيود], **Ṭayū** [طيو], **Ṭayūsh** [طيوش], **Hayṭayah** [هيطيه], **Lawraqash** [لورقش], **Ṣaṣlayahūrash** [صصليهورش]. **Answer**, **O Maymūn** [ميمون], **and you**, **O Bilāl** [بلال], **by the right of these names**.

Ninth Secret: **For Ḥāmand** [حامند] **and Qaṭrabah** [قطربه], **in Indian**. **Say**: **Adam** [ادم], **Am** [ام], **Mastadhkarah** [مستذكره], **Ḥāmandī** [حامندي], **Yūsh** [كوش], **Kayāl** [كيال], **Aqshar** [اقشر], **Hashar** [هشر], **Dī** [دي], **Dī** [دي], **Rī** [ري], **Rī** [ري], **Yā Yaklam** [يا يكلم], **Kal** [كل], **Kal** [كل], **Ham** [هم], **Ham** [هم], **Kal** [كل], **Kal** [كل], **Basharshūsh**

[بشرشوش]. **Answer forthwith, O Ḥāmand** [حامند] **and Qaṭrabah** [قطربه], **by the right of these names**.

Tenth Secret: **For Farṭīshā** [فرطيشا], **in Indian. Say**: **Aqrāh** [اقراه], **Aqrāh** [اقراه]; **Qaymā** [قيما], **Qaymā** [قيما]; **Kahshā** [كهشا], **Kahshā** [كهشا]; **Ṭashī** [طشي], **Ṭashī** [طشي]; **'Abathī** [عبثي], **'Abathī** [عبثي]; **Ghāshī** [غاشي]; **by thy Lord**; **Ash** [اش]; **Asham** [اشم]; **Shawā** [شوا]; **Asbaqāhayāl** [اسبقاهيال]; **Shawā** [شوا]; **Yashmā** [يشما]; **Khafūsh** [خفوش], **Khafūsh** [خفوش]; **Famā** [فما]; **Sarhā** [سرها], **Aqnūṭā** [اقنوطا]; **El**, **El**; **Shaddi**; **Khaj**, **Khaj**, **Khaj**, **Khaj**; **Astamar** [استمر]; **Khajaj** [خجج]. **"It is from Solomon**, **and it is in the name of the Divine**, **Most Merciful and Compassionate**, **saying**, **"Be not ye arrogant against me**, **but come ye unto me subservient**.'"

Eleventh Secret: **For 'Umar ibn Jābir** [عمر بن جابر], **in Indian. Say**: **Shadmasharah** [شدمشره], **Shadmayash** [شدميش], **Rawmash** [رومش], **Faqdas** [فقدس], **'Ūnayash** [عونيش], **Mūyadarsh** [مويدرش], **Qak'ash** [قكعش], **Qayūsh** [قيوش], **Quddūs** [قدوس], **Qaṭrāsh** [قطراش], **Halqash** [هلقش], **Qaṭrāsh** [قطراش], **Dayāyāsh** [ديا ياش], **'Asharāsh** [عشراش], **Wajūshīr** [وجوشير], **Dūshīr** [دوشير], **'Arūsh** [عروش], **Tarūsh** [تروش], **'Ūnayash** [عونيش], **Darūnayash** [درونيش], **Qayṭash** [قيطش], **Dajlafī** [دجلفي], **Laytāsh** [ليتاش]. **Haste**, **O 'Umar ibn Jābir** [عمر بن جابر], **by the right of the names**.

Twelfth Secret: **For Mahāqīl** [مهاقيل]. **This is in Indian, and is for conjuring. Say**: **Shakashā** [شكشا], **Mahāqāl** [مهاقال], **Mayah** [ميه], **Mandam** [مندم], **Barmandam** [برممندم], **Barmayah** [برميه] **O Zawba'ah** [زوبعة]! **Faqīm** [فقيم], **Lahā** [لها], **Fāqir** [فاقر], **Shamūkām** [شموكم], **Kashar** [كشر], **Lahā** [لها], **Aksar** [اكسر]. **O Da'nash** [دعنش] **and Da'ūsh Kawkahā** [دعوش كوكها]! **I am the messenger of Solomon. I conjure you, by the right of the Creator and the seal which encircles you; by the right which Mara'ūshā** [مرعوشا] **has over ye, O Mahāqīl** [مهاقيل]; **by the right which Kajlash Ṭaljāsh** [كجلش طلجاش] **has over ye, O Shamwīl** [شمويل]; **by the right which 'Aytūl** [عيطول] **has over ye, O Zawba'ah** [زوبعة]; **and by the right that Marṭayūsh** [مرطيوش] **has over ye, O Dahnash** [دهنش], **to come unto me from wheresoever ye hear me, from the places unto which ye are devoted. "Those who oppose Allah and His messenger shall be among the lowest. God has decreed: 'I will most certainly prevail, I and my messengers.' Indeed, the Divine is strong and almighty." Jarash** [جرش], **Sharash** [شرش], **Shayraṭash** [شيرطش], **Hatūr** [هتور], **Yā Sakh** [يا سخ]! **Ra'ūb** [رعوب], **Shaṭamūth** [شطموث], **Ba'dīd** [بعديد], **Fayūkh** [فيوخ], **Dawkatay** [دوكتي], **Wakazbayā** [وكزبيا]. **By Yā Shaflīf Shafāhā** [يا شفليف شفاها], **haste, haste. I conjure you, O company of four kings, by the right of these names, to answer obediently and quickly, by the leave of the Lord of the Worlds.**

The Secret Of The Spiritual Beings In Charge Of The Nights And Days, As Extracted From The Books Of Mysteries By Asaph The Son Of Berechiah

He said, "If you wish to undertake an important task that is difficult for you, then recite these names and say whatever you will and it will be accomplished quicker than the flash of lightning. Utter them only in in a state of cleanliness. These are the names: Awmathīkh Namū [اومثيق نمو] (**x**211), **Abshakhaythā** [ابشخيثا], **Maṣamaythā** [مصميثا], **Awmathīkh** [اومثيق], **Abaṭūshī** [ابطوشي], **Yā Lākhā** [يا لاخا], **Awmathīkh** [اومثيق], **Ṭūlā** [طولا], **Naydah** [نيده], **Awmathīkh** [اومثيق], **Bashkhaytathā** [بشخيتثا], **Nalnatā** [نلنتا], **Awmathīkh** [اومثيخ], **Yahmū** [يهمو], **Ṭawār** [طوار], **Hathaythā** [هثيثا], **Alahī** [الهي], **Faynaẓar** [فينظر], **Awmathīkh** [اومثيخ], **Bahāy** [بهاي], **Alahā** [الها], **Rayāṭālak** [رياطالك], **Yarhan** [يرهن], **Mareāl** [مرتال], **Hānī** [هاني], **Madshān** [مدشان], **Mashalayshākh** [مشليشاخ], **Baqshaṭā** [بقشطا], **Ta'tata'laf** [تعتعلف], **Alūkh** [الوخ], **Barayqawāsh** [بريقواش], **Malākhā** [ملاخا], **Alahā** [الها], **Lāwayt** [لاويت], **Awrātakī** [اوراتكي], **Qaṭlā** [قطلا], **Yaqṭalakh** [يقطلخ], **Amīn** [امين], **Amīn** [امين]."

The Names With Which The Lord Created The Seven Planets

The sage Ma'ādayūs said, "These are the names with which God created the seven planets."

First Secret: **For Saturn. You say**: **Hākh** [هاخ], **Lūkhākh** [لوخاخ], **Bashālikh** [بشالخ], **Maklahīkh** [مكلهيخ], **Quddūs** [قدوس], **Quddūs** [قدوس], **Lord of the angels and the Spirit**. **Answer ye me**, **by the right of these pure names**!

Second Secret: **For Jupiter. You say**: **Ṭakh** [طخ], **Ghāmi'** [غامض], **Jaymad** [جيمد], **Kandaryūd** [كندريود], **Knower of all things before they exist**. **Hasten**, **O inhabitants of Jupiter**!

Third Secret: **For Mars. You say**: **Karūnāy** [كروناي], **Jahārash** [جهارش], **Jahmarash** [جهمرش], **Shafī'** [شفيع], **Ṭīṭ** [طيط]. **O inhabitants of Mars**, **answer me obediently**.

Fourth Secret: **For the Sun. You say**: **"Blessed is the Light of Light**, **the Director of Affairs**. **O Hīkh** [هيخ], **O Hīkh** [هيخ], **Yāh** [ياه], **Yāh** [ياه]. **Hasten**, **O inhabitants of the Sun**!

Fifth Secret: **For Venus. You say**: **"Khajaḥ** [خجح], **Haylākh** [هيلاخ], **Maklāj** [مكلاج], **Ṭahshayrah** [طهشيره]. **O Venus**! **Hasten**, **O Zawba'ah al-Dhirā'** [زوبعة الذراع]!

Sixth Secret: **For Mercury. You say**: **Has** [هث], **Has** [هث], **Sharat** [شرت], **Marat** [مرت], **Ayrat** [ايرت], **Aywalat** [أيولت]. **Hasten**, **O Burqān** [برقان].

Seventh Secret: **For the Moon. You say**: **Aṣānayā** [اصانيا], **A'ākayā** [اعاكيا], **Ahashtahā** [اهشتها], **Fā'almā** [فاعلما]. **Hasten**, **O Abya'** [أبيض], **by the right of these names**!

Spells Required For Making A Possessing Spirit Manifest Himself In Dire Situations

With the grace and aid of the Lord, **we shall begin with the following**: **If someone brings a possessed person to you**, **and**

you wish to make his possessing jinni manifest himself, ask about his condition. If they say that he has seizures and speaks, or that he has seizures but his mouth does not contort, you know that it is a genuine Wind from among the jinn. If they say that he has seizures but does not contort, or that a sour-smelling vomit ejects from him, you know that it is one of the phlegmatic spirits and not a Wind from among the jinn; it is of nature. If you hear that he has seizures at the start or end of the night while he is standing, then know that his nature is composed of black bile. If you hear that he has seizures while he is awake, on the odd days of the start of the month—the third, fifth, seventh, or ninth—then know that it is from al-Thawkhab (the spell and remedy for which will come shortly, Allah Most High willing). If, when he has seizures, he does not drool, his vision is good, he lowers his gaze, and bows his head, it is definitely a jinni; so begin his treatment, and seek help for him from the Divine—the Creator is God. Sit the possessed person down alone and write the following names on his palm and the spirit will manifest himself, regardless of who he is.

Asaph the son of Berechiah said, "When the Pact was revealed to Solomon by the Divine, Mighty and Majestic, every king dictated his pledge, seal, pact, amulet, cure, and reproval to him. If you seek spells from Solomon the son of David for making a possessing jinni manifest himself, I have not seen a spell as good as this one dictated to him, which employs the pentacle."

Asaph the son of Berechiah said, "If a Wind comes to you from among the seven classes of spirits—the Danāhishah [دناهشة], Shawākhibah [شواخبة], or [فرزوقات] Farzūqāt—take a washtub and write therein the following names, wash them off with water that neither sunlight nor moonlight has touched, and place it inside a clean, pure, and furnished house censed with all kinds of fragrant smells. Only write them after sundown. Thereafter cense the washtub with aloeswood, nadd, frankincense, amber, camphor, and costus, and place it on three raw bricks, as it is better. Then recite the Syriac Conjuration over it three times and say, 'O company of kings, come to my home, so that I may seek your help for things of which the Lord Most High approves.' On that night, close the door of the house; on the following day, open it. Cast a circle large enough for you to sit in; burn incense, and recite the conjurations, with the seals written on a clean parchment before you. Then ask the possessed person to enter the house and his possessing jinni will manifest. Do likewise for anyone who is feverish, tongue-tied, imprisoned, or afflicted by a Wind. Then have him swear a covenant with him in the manner I have taught you, and do not hasten to kill him. Likewise, if a possessing jinni comes to you, write these words for him on his palm:

ا ه ا ه ا ه ا ه ا ه ا ه ا ه ا ه ا ه ا ه ا ه ا ه ١٩ ٢١ ططا ه ا ▽ ▽ لح

ا سر كل عمله طلسطلحكاطم حسكسطسلقفلد لملوه

سسعكعسه صحح ١٢ ٩ ه ه ١ ١١١ ك ١١ ك حم عسق

"Thus does God, Almighty and Wise, reveal unto you and unto those before you. Fī [في], Rash [رش], Sa'dawā [سعدوا], Balasūlakh [بلسولخ], Lakh [لخ], Lakh [لخ], Lakh [لخ]. Hasten ye, wheresoever ye may be, hastily! Jarjar [جرجر], Lakh [لخ], Lakh [لخ], Lakh [لخ], Lakh [لخ]. Hear ye and hasten by these names and that which they hold!

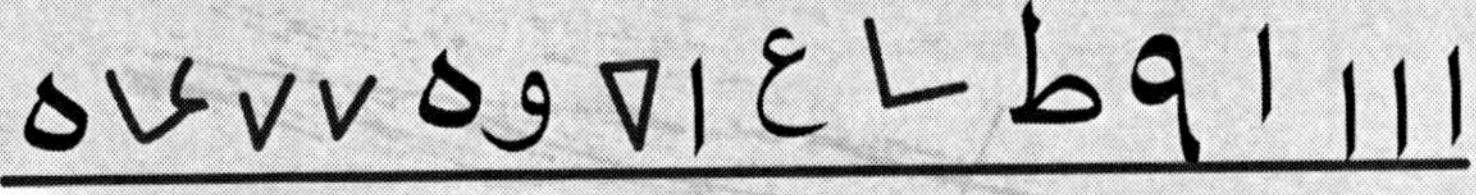

Hasten, hasten, O company of kings! Obey!"

Asaph the son of Berechiah said, "Following is the manner in which Solomon would make any possessing spirit manifest. In summary, you write the following names on a possessed person's palm and tell him to look at at it and this will force his possessor to manifest in a most violent manner. We know this as Ṣar' al-Akhtafaanah. You also recite them to the possessed person. They are as follows:

Kashalaqṭahā [كشلقطها], Ṭah [طه], Hayṭālūsh [هيطالوش], Maṭrayūsh [مطريوش], Kamshārash [كمشارش]. The light from the passing clouds shone. Make his possessing spirit manifest, by Mashtaṣīr [مشتصير], Nūfayl [نوفيل], 'Ashṭayl [عشطيل], Ehieh Asher Ehieh, Mālūkhā [مالوخا], Shaṭī [شطي], Shaṭyāl [شطيال]. O Rūkh [روخ], O Rūkhā, make his possessing spirit manifest, by the right of the names written upon the forehead of Isrāfīl [إسرافيل]: Salqaḥ [سلقح], Ṣa'aṣ, Shaltayūsh [شلتيوش], Ṭalṭaylash

[طلطيلش], **Mahlūshakh** [مهلوشخ], **Bahamīsh** [بهميش], **Rayhamayūsh** [ريهميوش], **Shahyah** [شهية], **Shahyah** [شهية], **Shayhash** [شيهش], **Ṭahash** [طهش], **Ṣaṭfakh** [سطفخ], **Shahūsh** [شهوش], **Haqlaytash** [هقليتش], **Tamhātayā** [تمهاتيا], **Dahash** [دهش], **Faham** [فهم], **Aghayūnā** [اغيونا]. **Hasten ye, by the right of these names. Then blow on his face and his possessing spirit will be made to manifest.**"

Discourse On The Carpet

Including, its uses, its benefits, instructions on how to use it in the circles, circle casting, the setting of seals out under the stars, and instructions on how to use this noble group pleasant to the spiritual sciences.

Know that only through its conditions, directions, and exercises, can one accomplish anything of the sciences. Therefore, keep your body and clothes clean, avoid sleep and eating unlawful food, and have awe of the Creator. As has been mentioned, use a carpet made of parchment, or of something else, such as a small tent,

on which you write the names mentioned at the beginning of the book. When you summon spirits while on the carpet, you shall be in either a desolate region or a house remote from any habitation. Let your spiritual exercise last for seven weeks, three weeks, or one week, which is the minimum. Whoever wishes to observe spiritual exercise shall by no means sleep at night, unless sleep overtakes him by force. Let him persist in reciting the conjuration. He should also be in a state of cleanliness, for he will see the spirits in his sleep, then in wakefulness. Let his sleep be in the daytime, from midmorning to noon; he should not sleep after midafternoon or dawn. Let him persist in asking forgiveness of the Lord and earnestly entreating Him. If your service is to a terrestrial or celestial servant from among the angels in charge of the Brilliant Planets, fashion the seal according to the planet's glyph, when the planet is in its exaltation, on its day, and let your clothing and carpet correspond to its color and incense. Lastly, let your conjuration be written on the previously mentioned carpet, for it will be more complete."

The one hundred names written on the front end:

'Awīl [عويل]; **'Azarīl** [عزريل]; **'Amānīl** [عمانيل]; **Ṣahṣahah** [صهصهة]; **Ṣamṣayūl** [صمصيول]; **Khaymash** [خيمش]; **Daymash** [ديمش]; **Hārish** [هارش]; **Qārish** [قارش]; **Ḥaydarash** [حيدرش]; **Khūṭṭāf** [خطاف]; **Jawlī** [جولي]; **Jamnahīsh** [جمنهيش]; **Jayd** [جيد]; **Nash** [نش]; **Qaysh** [قيش]; **Makhṭālīsh** [مخطاليش]; **Hayūlā** [هيولا]. **By**

Sha'lāsh [بشعلاش], **Mardāsh** [مرداش], **Qayūsh** [قيوش], **Ahlayl** [اهليل] , **Haybūt** [هيبوت], **Halyāwut** [هلياوت], **Awkhadī** [اوخدي], **Lāḥasan** [لاحسن], **Ṣatāṣīf** [صتاصيف], **Ahmaylakh** [اهميلخ], **Mahlūkh** [مهلوخ], **Damlūkh**, **Ṣardāsh** [صرداش], **Markūsh** [مركوش], **Ṭaqash** [طقش], **Shalāmīn** [شلامين], **Salām** [سلام], **Ah** [اه], **Wāh** [واه], **Yah** [يه], **Yahū** [يهو], **Shadah** [شده], **Shadah** [شده], **Jabarūt** [جبروت], **Jabarūt** [جبروت], **Jabrayānīl** [جبريانيل], **Ḥawrā** [حورا], **Salkaf** [سلكف], **Salkaf** [سلكف], **Salṭalaṭ** [سلطلط], **Shalṭā** [شلطا], **Maṭā** [مطا], **Makfakaf** [مكفكف], **Kaf** [كف], **Malakā** [ملكا], **Wabāghanī** [وباغني], **Bārīkh** [باريخ], **Qadayshā** [قديشا], **Ehieh Asher Ehieh**, **Abarīkh** [ابريخ], **Yārīkh** [ياريخ], **'Anī** [عني], **Bārīkh** [باريخ], **'Abarāt** [عبرات], **Bārīkh** [باريخ], **Baydalakh** [بيدلخ], **Bayrūkh** [بيروخ], **Basṭūr** [بسطور], **al-Nūr** [النور]— **"And verily it is a tremendous oath, if ye but knew."** **By Ḥā Mīm 'Ayn Sīn Qāf** [حم عسق]. **"The trumpet will be sounded, and all who are in the heavens and all who are in the earth will swoon except such as God wills.' 'And all will come to Him, humbled."** **By Kahaṭūl** [كهطول], **Malākh** [ملاخ], **Barākh** [براخ], **Ṭayshā** [طيشا], **Aḥmāḥamaythā** [احماحميثا], **Subbūḥ** [سبوح], **Quddūs** [قدوس], **Shaddi**, **'Awālīm** [عواليم], **Maṣarāyam** [مصرايم], **'Ash'āsh** [عشعاش], **Mardāsh** [مرداش], **Ṣaghrā** [صغرا], **Ramash** [رمش], **'Awālīsh** [عواليش], **Ṭamāghūsh** [ماغوش], **Hamalūqāsh** [هملوقاش], **Sa'ayrāsh** [صعيراش], **Tanash** [تنش], **Qaṭahar** [قطهر], **Qaṭāmīsh** [قطاميش], **Sha'qūsh** [شعقوش], **Razayūsh** [رزيوش], **'Ayūsh** [عيوش], **Daryūsh** [دريوش], **Qaybakāsh** [قيبكاش], **Ash** [اش], **Shamālūsh** [شمالوش], **'Aqmāyash**

[عقمايش], **Darmāyash** [درمايش], **Darmash** [درمش]. **Hasten**! **Hasten**!

The fifty noble, majestic names written on the right side:

Yahlayūh [يهليوه], **Karkayāṭ** [كركياط], **Hayūr** [هيور], **Kashayrayāwub** [كشيرياوب], **Ahmalīm** [اهمليم], **Sha'yahūsh** [شعيهوش], **Ḥawālīm** [حواليم], **'Abdalīm** [عبدليم], **Qasharaym** [قشريم], **Ṭūshalīm** [طوشليم], **Ṭūshāl** [طوشال], **'Alshāqash** [علشاقش], **Mahrāqīsh** [مهراقيش], **Ṭaqlā** [طقلا], **'Aqayl** [عقيل], **Habayd** [هبيد], **Rashwā** [رشوا], **Shaqīm** [شقيم], **Rafūsh** [رفوش], **Daqyāshīm** [دقياشيم], **Sarākhīl** [سراخيل], **Damāqīr** [دماقير], **Dahayūl** [دهيول], **Hū** [هو], **Hawṣayāl** [هوصيال], **Qūsh** [قوش], **Marayūsh** [مريوش], **Qayūsh** [قيوش], **Mārish** [مارش], **'Afkal** [عفكل], **Shaykal** [شيكل], **Shahāṭash** [شهاطش], **Yaklāwush** [يكلاوش], **Kal** [كل], **Wash** [وش], **Dayūsh** [ديوش], **Barkhārīsh** [برخاريش], **Jahah** [جهه], **Ṣafyah** [صفيه], **Jawdarah** [جودرة], **Marah** [مره], **Yūyah** [يويه], **Darāsh** [دراش], **Damhalājash** [دمهلاجش], **Ṭarūsh** [طروش], **Karūsh** [كروش], **Ḥayūm** [حيوم], **Qayyūm** [قيوم], **Ilāhā** [الها], **Rabbā** [ربا], **Qadīsā** [قديسا].

The fifty names written on the left side:

Abā [ابا], **Ilāhā** [الاها]. **By Sha'yādh** [شعياذ], **Yawraṭālash** [يورطالش], **Mahrāqash** [مهراقش], **Maykhā** [ميخا], **Ṭahaysh** [طهيش], **Ṭalash** [طلش], **Dar'āsh** [درعاش], **'Ashqash** [عشقش], **Tareīb** [ترتيب], **Marātīl**

[مراتيل], **Barhayūd** [برهيود], **Raqāyal** [رقايل], **Barqīl** [برقيل], **Wāsh** [واش], **Lamāsh** [لماش], **Ṭaqyāsh** [طقياش], **Ṭaymarūsh** [طيمروش], **Hārish** [هارش], **Lāwush** [لاوش], **Faṣaṣ** [فصص], **Ḥabarnab** [حبرنب], **Hawāṭīl** [هواطيل], **Kalkanūsh** [كلكنوش], **Rahūsh** [رهوش], **Arkayūsh** [اركيوش], **Dālish** [دالش] , **'Awlash** [عولش], **Wārayāsh** [وارياش], **Bahāsh** [بهاش], **'Awash** [عوش], **Yā 'Āsh** [يا عاش], **Yā Rāsh** [يا راش], **Wāsh** [واش], **Wārāsh** [واراش], **Warāsh** [وراش], **Nūsh** [نوش], **Nūsh** [نوش], **Ṣarṣarjayā** [صرصرجيا], **Yabarshūsh** [يبرشوش], **Barnayūsh** [برنيوش], **Dahyūsh** [دهيوش], **Radhab** [رذب], **'Ayānaq** [عيانق], **Mahwārash** [مهوارش], **Bahwārash** [بهوارش], **Dayūh** [ديوه], **Yūh** [يوه], **Māh** [ماه], **Yūlakh** [يولخ].

The names written on the back end:

O Creator, **by Your name Fay'ūj** [فيعوج], **Day'ūj** [ديعوج], **Bay'ūj** [بيعوج], **Shafāhā** [شفاها], **Sharalīsh** [شرليش], **Awyāh** [اوياه], **Baryāh** [برياه], **Dahūh** [دهوه], **Yah** [يه], **Yah** [يه], **Haylā** [هيلا], **Shamlā** [شملا], **Arkhayā** [ارخيا], **Ayāh** [اياه], **Markūsh** [مركوش], **Rūsh** [روش], **Ashyakh** [اشيخ], **Shakhaykh** [شخيخ], **Shāmikh** [شامخ], **Qaṭayṭ** [قطيط], **Maṭayṭ** [مطيط], **Sālūn** [سالون], **'Af'ash** [عفعش], **Ḥayf** [حيف], **Aqash** [اقش], **Maqash** [مقش], **Qarāyūsh** [قرايوش], **Darūsh** [دروش], **Barūshā** [بروشا], **Ahyūthā** [اهيوثا], **Shaksham** [شكشم]. **By Kasham** [كشم], **Rashīm** [رشيم], **Dayūq** [ديوق], **Māliq** [مالق], **'Alyā** [عليا], **Sham** [شم], **'Awāqīm** [عواقيم], **Mahyālayān** [مهياليان], **Thūb** [ثوب], **Tharehūb** [ثربوب], **Māsh** [ماش], **Qarākh** [قراخ], **Karākh** [كراخ], **Ḥayūrakh** [حيورخ], **Barhayā**

[برهيا], **Shamrāthā** [شمراثا], **Tabrāthā** [تبراثا], **Mālish** [مالش], **Jawlā** [جولا], **Ṭalmakh** [طلمخ], **Shala'** [شلع], **Faqṭashlakh** [فقطشلخ], **Mahṭīl** [مهطيل], **Hatīl** [هطيل], **Marṭīl** [مرطيل], **Haṭīl** [هطيل], **Yaṭal** [يطل], **Ṭawāshikh** [طواشخ], **Ṭalīkh** [طليخ], **Ḥa'lakh** [حعلخ], **Hayūt** [هيوت], **Hayūt** [هيوت], **Raqshayādah** [رقشياده], **Hāshā** [هاشا], **Lahyā** [لهيا], **Kasā** [كسا], **Ayqashān** [ايقشان], **Thabwā** [ثبوا], **Dayūh** [ديوه], **Bayāṣūm** [بياصوم], **Rabah** [ربه], **Darākh** [دراخ], **Marhālikh** [مرهالخ], **Bar'āsh** [برعاش], **Qarāsh** [قراش], **Mārish** [مارش], **Rādish** [رادش], **Ḥādish** [حادش], **Ṣaymar** [صيمر], **Hamyar** [همير], **Hasū** [هثو], **Tawghar** [توغر], **Ghūsh** [غوش], **Ghar'ayūsh** [غرعيوش], **'Āṣim** [عاصم], **Qāṣim** [قاصم], **Dā'ish** [داعش], **Far'ash** [فرعش], **Qalamūsh** [قلموش], **Qashra'ash** [قشرعش], **Qaysh** [قيش], **Awdayūsh** [اوديوش], **Laykūsh** [ليكوش], **Jayah** [جيه], **Jayhah** [جيهه], **Jayūlash** [جيولش], **Ṭahyānah** [طهيانه], **Ṭahūrah** [طهورة], **Aryāh** [ارياه], **Artayāyāh** [ارتياياه], **Qaydūl** [قيدول], **Tayārayāh** [تيارياه], **Rayāh** [رياه], **Dasham** [دشم], **Dasham** [دشم], **Markasham** [مركشم], **Ṣawn** [صون], **Yashrā** [يشرا], **Shalīm** [شليم], **Shalāmīn** [شلامين], **Sā'ūq** [صاعوق], **Nā'ūq** [ناعوق], **Lā'ij** [لاعج], **Mā'ij** [ماعج], **'Ajīj** [عجيج], **Ba'īj** [بعيج], **'Awādīm** [عواديم], **Ṣarnāyīm** [صرناييم], **Malākhīm** [ملاخيم], **Khalātūq** [خلاتوق], **Malākhūq** [ملاخوق], **Ṣa'jaf** [صعجف], **Mawājif** [مواجف], **Khafīf** [خفيف], **Jafjaf** [جفجف], **Jarīr** [جرير], **Ḥāyūr** [حايور], **Jāyūr** [جايور], **Laṭīf** [لطيف], **Qūrash** [قورش], **Qaṭarūsh** [قطروش], **Ṣayrā** [صيرا], **Hūmā** [هوما], **Ṭaqīsh** [طقيش], **Ṭaqrāsh** [طقرش], **Ṭaqāsh** [طقاش], **Hīsh** [هيش], **Harām** [هرام], **Kabrāṣ** [كبراص], **Damlāṣ** [دملاص], **Dalayṣ** [دليص], **Ḥaṣayṣ** [حصيص], **Ḥaylūnash**

[حيلونش], **Ṭaqmash** [طقمش], **Ṭawāsh** [طواش], **Ṭahqīsh** [طهقيش], **Ḥawāh** [حواه], **Karayd** [كريد], **Yāṣūrā** [ياصورا], **Ḥūdā** [حودا], **Yākhān** [ياخان], **Damaylā** [دميلا], **Khān** [خان], **Akhān** [اخان], **Jabarūn** [جبرون], **Jayrāwūn** [جيراوون], **Jabarāwūt** [جبراووت], **Jabarāwūt** [جبراووت], **Qarmānish** [قرمانش], **Qarmayāsh** [قرمياش], **Marmaynāmīn** [مرمينامين], **'Alāmīn** [علامين], **Al'azayā** [العزيا], **Qarqarūn** [قرقرون], **Malshayā** [ملشيا], **Shayūr** [شيور], **Mashtār** [مشتار], **Sayūkh** [سيوخ], **Quddūs** [قدوس], **Saqalūṭ** [سقلوط], **Lājīn** [لاجين], **Ṣarājīn** [صراجين], **Ṣawāmīn** [صوامين], **Arkāsh** [اركاش], **Rakūsh** [ركوش], **Kaymūsh** [كيموش], **Hamā'ayūsh** [حماعيوش], **Abaraydaq** [ابريدق], **Mālāqīm** [مالاقيم], **Jabarāhīm** [جبراهيم], **Hamqāsh** [همقاش], **Ṭawālīsh** [طواليش], **'Amalūsh** [عملوش], **'Amqālīsh** [عمقاليش], **'Awdayāl** [عوديال], **Dayāl** [ديال], **Kareahūsh** [كرتهوش], **Fayqaṭūsh** [فيقطوش], **Darash** [درش], **Darwayūsh** [درويوش], **Ṣahrām** [صهرام], **'Awām** [عوام], **Ṣayhayūsh** [صيهيوش], **Ṭahrām** [طهرام], **'Arām** [عرام], **Ṣayhūsh** [صيهوش].

On it you say the names that are at the beginning of the book, the names with which the angels of the Throne and the Footstool along with the inhabitants of the seven firmaments glorify God, which, as we have said, we cited at the beginning of the book. You recite them while in the prescribed state I have written about for you, which entails adherence to religion and absolute conviction. Thereupon all the Ruhaniyyah will be unveiled to you and you will attain your objective in both this world and the hereafter. Let your summoning of the angels and the celes-

tial and terrestrial spirits and their habitations be for the fulfillment of your needs and for the seeking of their aid against your enemies and those of God Most High.

Commentary On The Twelve Names

They are the Supreme Names by which the Divine distinguished Moses and Joshua the son of Nun, who invoked God Most High therewith, whereupon the sun stood still for him.

The first name is "Bism Dasazāʿīl Dawkhashīm [باسم دسزائيل دوخشيم]," which means, "The angels fell upon their faces from the light of the glory of Your name, O my God." It is the name with which the Lord created the angels who are in charge of the regions of the earth.

The second name is "Makthādūshīm [مخثادوشيم]," which means, "How glorious is Your name, O Creator! Blessed are You and highly exalted."

The third name is "Bism Hūlaym [باسم هوليم]," which means, "You, You, O He who dazzles with this extraordinary power."

The fourth name is "'Aymāqawīl Salkhūth [عوماقويل سلخوث]," which means, "By the right of this name, help You Your servants!" Thereupon twelve springs gushed forth from the stone.

The fifth name is "Al-'Azīz al-Jabbār [العزيز الجبار]." By this name, He made the seas and rivers to flow.

The sixth name is "Hawālīm Shaṭūrīm [هواليم شطوريم]," which means, "the almighty and wise Lord."

The seventh name is "Mashīm Alhūkhā [مشيم الهوخا]," which means, "The exalted and highest God who is free of need from any creature."

The eighth name is "'Ashāqīm Daykam Shaṭūrīm [عشاقيم ديكم شطوريم]," which means, "The angels fell prostrate from Your glory, O my God. You are Lord of the Worlds."

The ninth name is "Salkhūth Rakīm El Ṣayrakh [سلخوث ركيم ال صيرخ]," which means, "In the name of Him whose command the heavens and the earth obey, the Possessor of Majesty and Generosity."

Recite the names after saying the following hymnic invocation: "O Ḥannān [حنان], O Mannān [منان],

O Ṭāhir [طاهر], O Muṭahhir [مطهر], there is no god but You. O He who is possessed of sovereignty, power, honor, and might; O He who is clothed with dignity and light and clad in bounty and generosity, the Almighty, the Oft-forgiving, there is no god but You. You give life and death, exalt and abase, and have power over all things. By Your name Salkhūth Rakīm El Ṣayrakh [سلخوث ركيم ال صيرخ].

The tenth name is "Layākhīm [لياخيم]," which means, "You are God, the King, the Subduer, the Originator of the heavens and the earth."

The eleventh name is "Layālaghū [ليالغو]," which means, "the praised God."

The twelvth name is "Ba'alnā Rayt [بعلنا ريت]," which means, "God, the Guardian, the Omniscient."

This concludes the secrets. Their origin is as follows: Ayā Raygh Layārūsh Layāshalash [ايا ريغ ليارو ش لياشلش]. They are useful for driving away contagion and famine. To do that, take a cup filled with milk and a cup filled with honey, place them on your property when the Sun enters the first minute of Aries, and say: "O Creator, by Your most glorious names and Your supreme words that you said to all things—'Be!'— whereupon that which You willed to happen happened, drive contagion and famine away from us. Surely You are able to do all things."

Know that each of these names has a usage, along with angels charged to fulfill needs. If you wish to use them for things pertaining to the rūḥāniyyah who dwell on Earth, then recite the names and say, "O noble angels, by the right of these magnificent names, I adjure you to command the spirit so and so to do such and such" and he will do what you wish. You can only perform these usages in this manner.

The First Usage: When you wish to travel by land, recite the name and say, "O angels in charge of this route, by the right of this glorious, blessed, honorable name, do not leave me until I return unto my homeland, and be with me for the fulfillment of my needs." They will aid you and stay with you, and you will remain protected wherever you go, by the permission of God Most High.

The Second Usage: When you wish to travel by sea, recite the foregoing name and say, "O angels in charge of this sea, by the name with which El divided the sea for Moses, I adjure you to help me traverse this sea and protect me against its evil, that I may disembark as quickly as possible and be spared from its evil and the evil of its waves." You will, by the permission of God Most High, travel in safety, with ease, and quickly, and you will see neither evil nor misfortune.

The Third Usage: If you encounter robbers or beasts of prey on the road or on a journey, take a handful of dirt from the land you are on, recite the name over it, and say, "O angels in charge of the land, by the right this name has over you, I entreat you to protect me from their evil." They will be overcome before you by the permission of the Lord Most High.

The Fourth Usage: If someone brings a possessed person to you, take a cup, pour limpid water therein, recite the names over it twenty-one times, and say, "O angels, angels of this name, surrender to me the demon of so and so." They will hand him over to you, and the possessed person's cure will be by the permission of God Most High.

The Fifth Usage: If a man comes to you bound, so that he cannot have intercouse with his wife, then take either water from a well untouched by sunlight, rainwater or water from a stone well and recite the name over it. Then say, "O angels in charge of bodily parts and senses, I adjure you by the right these names has over you to unbind so-and-so the son of so-and-so (Insert the first name of the female parent, hereafter referred to as f.)." Then have the person perform an ablution with such water and drink of it. His unbinding will be by the permission of the Lord Most High.

Sixth Usage: If a woman whose children are dying from Stalker Jinn comes to you, make four tin plates for her. Inscribe the name on top of and under each plate, and say, "O all ye Stalker Jinn who are seizing the children of so-and-so the daughter of so-and-so (f.), by the right of this name, remain not in this city or country or house a moment longer. Depart unto the idol worshippers and him who invokes another di-ety in addition to the Creator." Then bury the plates in the four corners of the house and the Stalker Jinn will leave her and her cure will be by the permission of the Lord Most High.

Seventh Usage: If someone has been in prison for a long time, take dirt from the prison, mix it with egg whites, and make a potsherd out of it. Then write the name on it, go to a beach, throw it in the water, and say, "Just as this dirt has left the prison and ended up in the sea, so too will so-and-so the son of so-and-so (f.) leave his prison, by the leave of God Most High."

Eighth Usage: If you wish to hear from some-one who is away, then say, after peforming the prayer, "O angels in charge of (here you name the direction you know the person is in), bring me N. the son of N. (f.)." They will come to you and bring you the person, and you will receive information from him.

Ninth Usage: If you wish to fulfill a difficult need, fashion a figure out of white wax and stand it in front of you. Then cense the front of it with mastic and aloeswood, recite the name, and say, "O angels in charge of N. the son of N. (f.), bring me N. the son of N. (f.)" and they will bring him to you.

Tenth Usage: If you wish to annihilate one of your enemies, make a hollow figure of him out of

lead and inscribe its chest with his name. Then stand it in front of you in your sanctuary. When you are finished with your prayer, summon the angels in charge of the entire body and limbs of N., son of N. (f.), saying, "O all ye angels in charge of this person, do ye approve of N. being empowered over this person? Let them bring a bearer of witness and one against whom the witness will be borne." Thereupon two of the Angels of Wrath will come to you. Say to them, "Be ye empowered over him who is represented by this figure, and demote him." Then cast the figure into a fire and it will destroy him and spare people from his evil.

Following are the names of the angels in charge of the first name.

Say: **Sharāṭīl** [شراطيل], **Samā'īl** [سمائيل], **Hayā'īl** [هيائيل], **Ṭafyā'īl** [طفيائيل], **Rūqayā'īl** [روقيائيل], **Mīkhayā'īl** [ميخيائيل], **Karsayā'īl** [كرسيائيل], **Gharbayā'īl** [غربيائيل].

Commentary On The Name Of Clouds

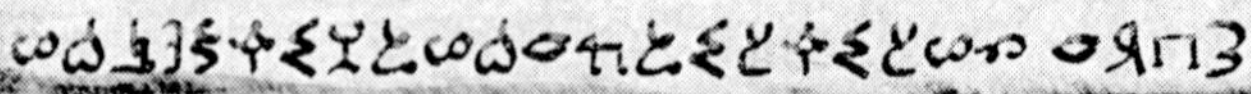

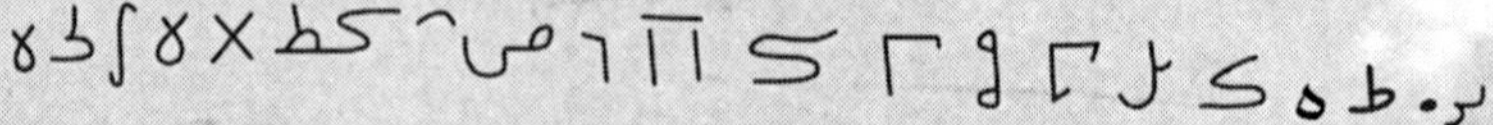

This is the name with which the Lord Most High created the clouds and the angels who are in charge of them and who glorify God in their planets. All the angels—there are ten of them—must obey this name. Say:

Sarfayā'īl [سرفيائيل], **Dardayā'īl** [درديائيل], **Sam'ayā'īl** [سمعيائيل], **Arqayā'īl** [ارقيائيل], **Hamyatā'īl** [هميتائيل], **Samsamā'īl** [سمسمائيل], **Jamjayā'īl** [جمجيائيل], **Asahrayāl** [اسهريال], **Ṣamṣamayāl** [صمصميال], **Ḥarqayāl** [حرقيال].

Second Usage: **If you wish to make it rain on a summer day**, **sit out in the open and recite the following names**. **After reciting them for an hour**, **clouds will come**. **If there is delay in their coming**, **recite the names a second time and say**, **"O noble angels**, **make it rain." They will order the angels in charge of the sea to create clouds**, **at which time it will rain**. **The usage of this name**

gave the children of Israel rain to drink.

Third Usage: If you wish there to be thunder at a time unbefitting it, recite the names and say, "O angel in charge of thunder, I adjure ye by the right of this name to bring thunder."

Fourth Usage: If an ill person choked by a possessing jinni, a hemiplegic, or someone afflicted by a Wind from among the dwellers of the clouds comes to you, recite this name over clean water and give it to him to drink and his cure will be by the permission of the Lord Most High. Moreover, utter the names of the ten angels, for whatever you use them for will be successfull by the permission of God Most High.

Fifth Usage: If you wish to have a spirit or one of the angels inhabiting the clouds brought to you, recite this name and say, "Bring me the angel N." He will appear before you faster than the blink of an eye. Give any command you wish and he will obey it, by the permission of the Lord Most High.

Sixth Usage: If you wish to have books transported from one country to another, recite the name along with the names of the previously mentioned angels and say, "Let him who can fulfil my need come." They will bring to you from among the inhabitants of the clouds one who can fulfill your need and throw the book into the home of whomever you wish.

Seventh Usage: If you wish to stone a person's home, recite the name along with the names of the previously mentioned angels and say, "Let there come unto me from among the inhabitants of the clouds one who will stone the home of N." They will obey your command by the permission of God Most High.

Eighth Usage: If you wish to annihilate any of the Creator's tyrannical enemies from among the rebellious transgressors, or depose powers, servants, and the like, recite the name and then the previously mentioned angelic names. They will do whatever you desire by the permission of God Most High.

Ninth Usage: For the fulfillment of needs in faraway lands, say the name and the angels following it and then command as you wish and they will do it.

Tenth Usage: For the manifestation of any spirit.

Commentary On The Name Of Winds

These are ten Names with which God created the wind and subjected it to Solomon the son of David, gently carrying him with it wherever it went, and with which He Most High sent a cold wind against the people of 'Ād, annihilating them.

They are the following ten: Sandabā'īl [سندبائيل], **Shahrakā'īl** [شهركائيل], **Haḥamkīn** [هحمكين], **Ahwākīl** [اهواكيل], **Ṣarfayā'īl** [صرفيائيل], **Hamrākīl** [همراكيل], **Arqīl** [ارقيل], **Ahjamlayā'īl** [اهجمليائيل], **Asrākayṭayā'īl** [اسراكيطيائيل], **and Ahrākīl** [اهراكيل]. **These are the names of the ten angels.**

First Usage: If you want to capsize the ship of any enemy of the Lord Most High you wish, stand on a beach, take some of its mud, recite over it the name along with the names of the angels, throw it into the ocean, and say, "O angels, I adjure you by the power of the name to overturn N's ship." Thereupon the sea will foam and surge and the ship will capsize by the permission of God Most High.

Second Usage: If you wish to travel by sea and return safely, by the permission of the Lord Most High, recite the name and say, "O angels, I desire from you a wind for the ship." A wind will come to you by which you will reach your destination, covering three days' distance in a single day, and you will be protected against the terror of the sea.

Third Usage: If you wish to remove a tyrant, fashion a hollow figure in his likeness out of white wax and write the name on its chest. Then stand the figure up using two packing needles driven into the floor and say, "O angels of El in charge of domination and punishment, be empowered over N. the son of N. (f.), by the right this name has over you." Then sever any of the figure's limbs you wish and he will perish by the permission of God Most High.

Fourth Usage: If an ailing person choked by a possessing jinni or a hemiplegic comes to you, recite the before mentioned names and say, "Expel this evil Wind from N." and he will come out by the permission of the Lord Most High.

Fifth Usage: If a woman is having difficulty giving birth, then write the names of the angels along with the name and give it to her to drink and she will deliver quickly.

Sixth Usage: If you have proposed to a woman whom it is difficult for you to marry, invoke God Most High with the name and call out the names of the angels. He will make marriage to her easy for you, by the blessing of the names of Him Most High.

Seventh Usage: If you wish to walk on water, fast for three days according to your spiritual excercise. Then go to a sea and say the name along with the names of the angels and the Lord Most High will carry you over the sea and you will walk on it as if was the ground.

Eighth Usage: If you wish to cross the distance of a year's journey in a single night, take a piece of cloth, write the name in the center of it and encircle it with the names of the angels. Sit on it cross-legged, facing your destination, and say, "Take me to such and such place," and you will arrive there.

Ninth Usage: If you wish to make someone who is not present come to you, write the name along with the said names and hang it up. He will come by the permission of God Most High.

Tenth Usage: If you want to make a spring gush forth from anywhere in the ground you wish, recite the name and call the angel in charge of the ground. Water will gush forth for you by the permission of the Lord Most High.

The Shamkhuthi Names

Say: **Shamkhaythā** [شمخيثا], **Shalmakhūthā** [شلمخوثا], **Haythakhā** [هيثخا], **Aythakhyā** [ايثخيا], **Aythakhaythā** [ايثخيثا], **Halaythamkhā** [هليثمخا], **Tarūkhā** [تروخا], **Barūkhā** [بروخا], **Samyāthā** [سمياثا], **Samyāyām** [سميايم], **Khathāyam** [ختايم], **Ehieh Asher Ehieh**, **Adonai Tzabaoth**, **Ṣahyāyūt** [صهيايوت]. **O El Shaddi**, **O Maṣqaṣ** [مصقص], **O Khālīkhā** [خاليخا], **O Badī** [بدي], **O Lūthā** [لوثا], **O Mashfaqa'īsh** [مشفقعيش], **O Hūyāl** [هويال], **O Lūhāyim** [لوهايم], **O Lūhīm** [لوهيم], **O Zakhabīlā** [زخبيلا], **O Lūthā** [لوثا], **O Radabīlā** [ردبيلا], **O Raghabīlā** [رغبيلا], **O Ramā** [رما], **O 'Awlā** [عولا], **O Qarnāyā** [قرنايا], **O Wamāl** [ومال], **O Hayū Ehieh Māh Wayah** [هيو اهيه ماه ويه], **O Shanūth Shamlū'** [شنوث شملوع].

This concludes the names. Among the names is a glorious name with which the angels in heaven supplicate. It is "Yāhū Hūh [ياهو هوه]**"; some say it is "Yā Hūh** [يا هوه]**."**

Dismissal

Say: **Go ye, and depart, by the honor of Ashmakh** [اشمخ], **Shamkhā**, **Malīkh** [مليخ], **Ehieh Asher Ehieh, Adonai Tzabaoth, El Shaddi. The hand of the Creator is more open than the hand of the created. The hand of the Sustainer is stronger than the hand of the sustained. "The kindled fire of the Divine that rises above the heavens will verily be closed over them, in outstretched columns." I dismiss the angels of God and the inhabitants of the clouds and highest firmaments who are in charge of the secrets of the Lord of the Worlds. I dismiss them by all of the perfect and universal names of the Divine. "And Our command is but one, as the twinkling of an eye."**

Go ye, depart, by the right of Baṭfayārish [بطفيارش], **Ṭafyatūsh** [طفيتوش], **Shalhayūhash** [شلهيوهش], **Aljārish** [الجارش], **Yajūrat** [يجورت], **Hayārish** [هيارش], **Harshayūnah** [هرشيونه], **Ḥarmash** [حرمش], **Fayfarmash** [فيفرمش]. **Go ye, by the light of the countenance of the Lord, by which the heavens, the earth, and all that is therein radiate. That is the**

Creator. There is no god but Him, Lord of the majestic Throne.

The Glyphs Of The Seven Days

Write on paper on Sunday for Ruqayā'īl [روقيائيل]:

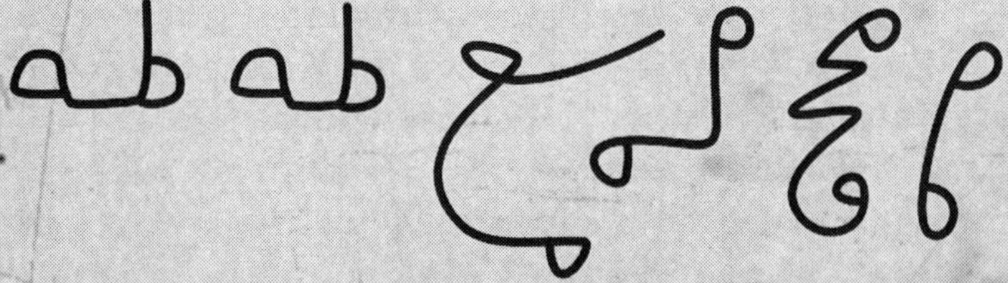

Write on paper on Monday for Jibrā'īl [جبرائيل]:

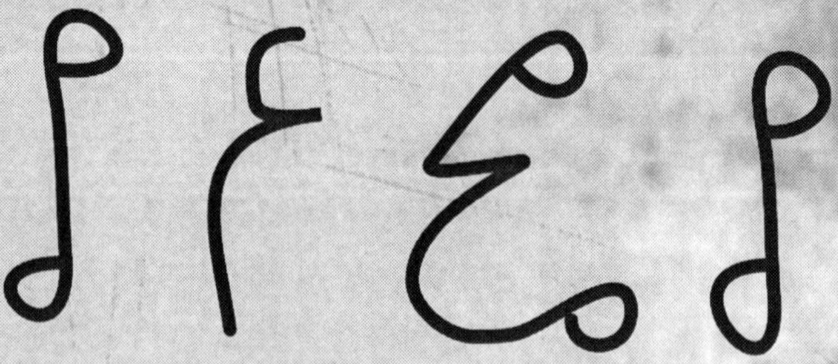

Write on paper on Tuesday for Samsamā'īl [سمسمائيل]:

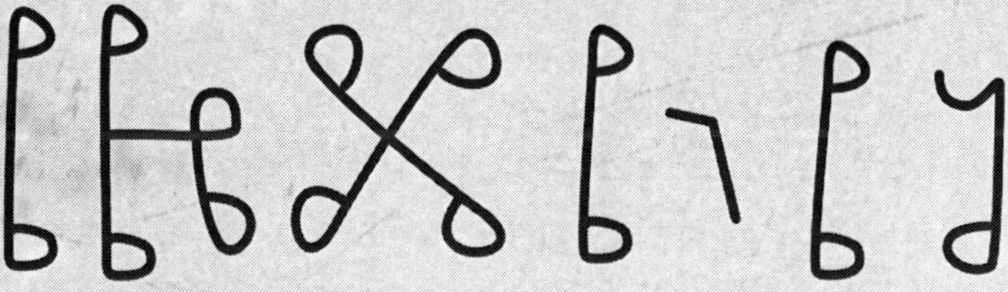

Write on paper on Wednesday for Mīkā'īl [ميكائيل]:

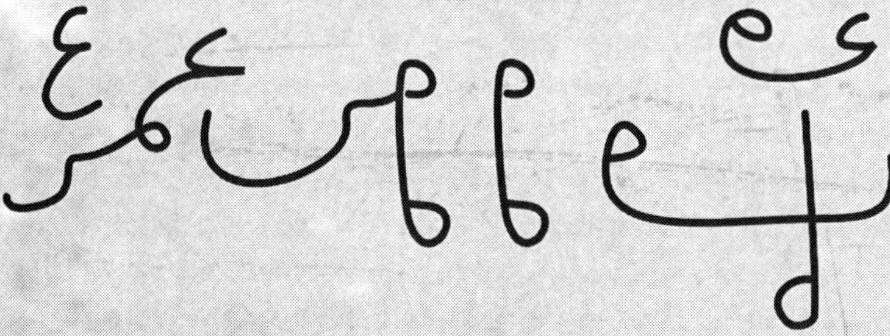

Write on paper on Thursday for Rūqayā'il [روقيائيل]:

Write on paper on Friday for 'Anyā'īl [عنيائيل]:

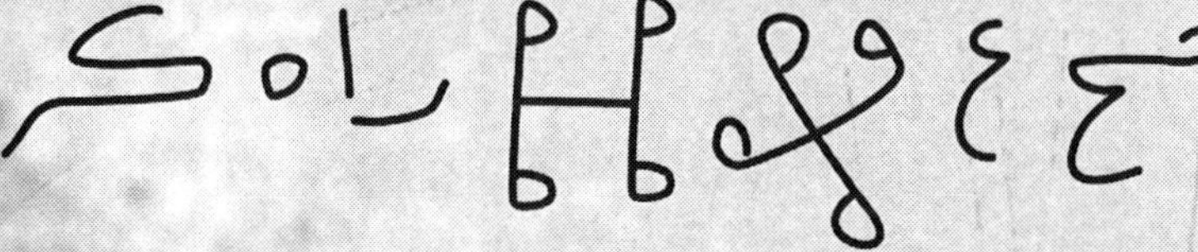

Write on paper on Saturday for Kasfayā'īl [كسفيائيل]:

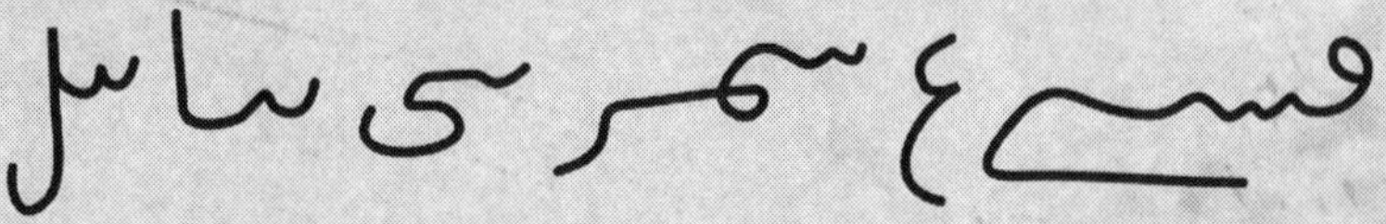

The First Name: Fashion a hollow figure in the likeness of whomever you wish out of sandarac and frankincense and on it write its corresponding glyphs. Write the names on a clean parchment using saffron, musk, and rosewater, place it inside the figure, and conjure them and the ruhani by the name. Write the previously mentioned name on its left leg and your name on its chest. It is for entering the presence of sovereigns, the fulfillment of needs, burning, and all jinn, the Earth, and countries.

The Second Name: Fashion it from silver and use it for entering the presence of sovereigns and leaders and for fulfilling needs.

The Third Name: It is for the bound.

The Fourth Name: Fashion it from white wax and use it for love, affection, and fulfilling needs.

The Fifth Name: Use it for exorcisms and the return of missing persons.

The Sixth Name: Fashion it from copper and use

it for assaulting, reproving, subduing, and killing others, for protection from fear and worry, and for seizing venomous creatures.

The Seventh Name: Fashion it from white wax and inscribe the glyphs on the center of the figure and the names on different parts of the body and on any place wherein is a Wind. Then stab any place where the Wind is, to obtain his cure. Make a wick and impregnate it with lily or ben tree oil. Light the wick at the top of the head. The Names of Killing are the Seven Secrets. Summon each angel by his Ruhaniyyah, and in his time and hour. Do not summon him by other than his Ruhaniyyah—understand this.

The Glyphs Of The Ruhaniyyah Employed On The Seven Days

The glyph of Sunday's Ruhaniyyah is

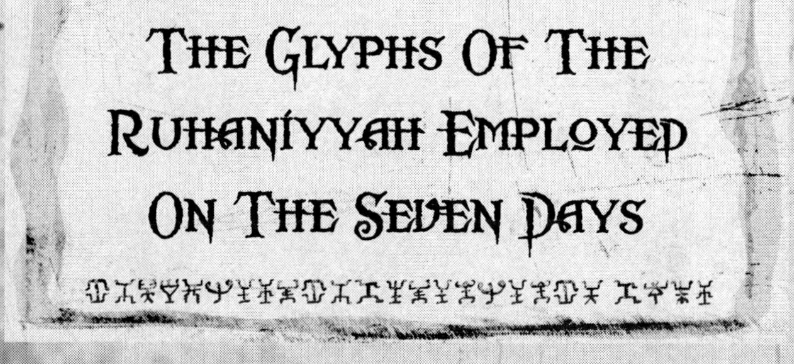

The glyph of Monday's Ruhaniyyah is امشاكلا

The glyph of Tuesday's Ruhaniyyah is الحمل ه ه

The glyph of Wednesday's Ruhaniyyah is كاملاها ه

The glyph of Thursday's Ruhaniyyah is اياهل

The glyph of Friday's Ruhaniyyah is سلا ياه

The glyph of Saturday's Ruhaniyyah is دهال يا طلاه

The Glyphs Of The Seven Terrestrial Kings

The glyph of Sunday's Terrestrial King is
ولي يا كف

The glyph of Monday's Terrestrial King is
الاعمرون وروف

The glyph of Tuesday's Terrestrial King is
ربي ودهوش

The glyph of Wednesday's Terrestrial King is
و ض ع ن

The glyph of Thursday's Terrestrial King is

من كمو و لا نه

The glyph of Friday's Terrestrial King is

وارح ستم

The glyph of Saturday's Terrestrial King is

بجهرس

The Glyphs of the Seven Brilliant Planets

Sunday: The glyph of the Sun is

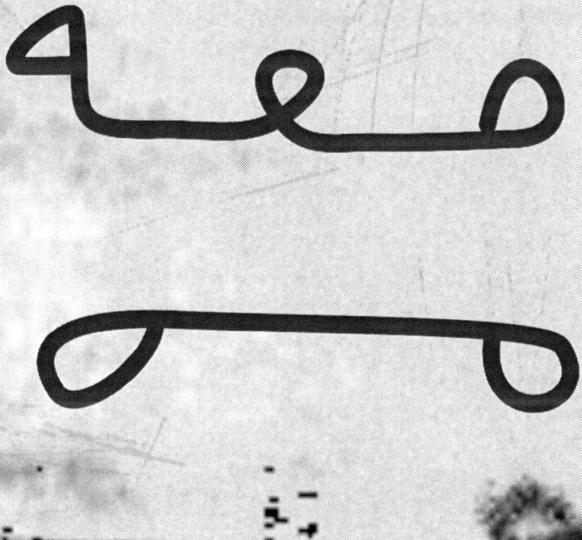

Monday: **The glyph of the Moon is**

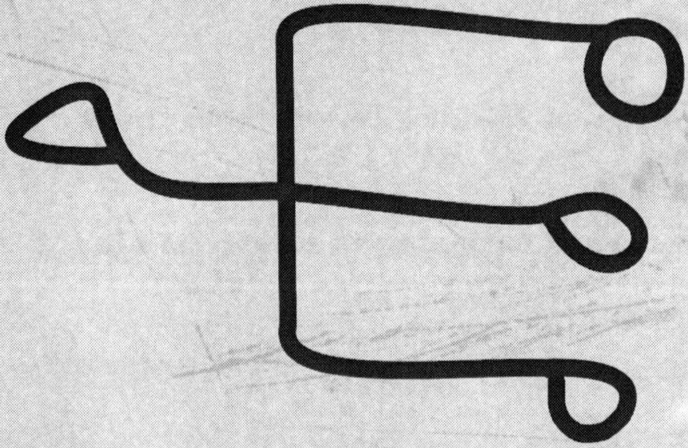

Tuesday: **The glyph of Mars is**

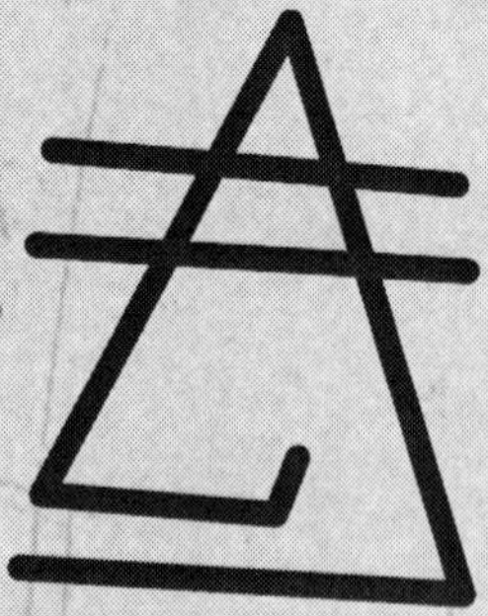

مصف

Wednesday: **The glyph of Mercury is**

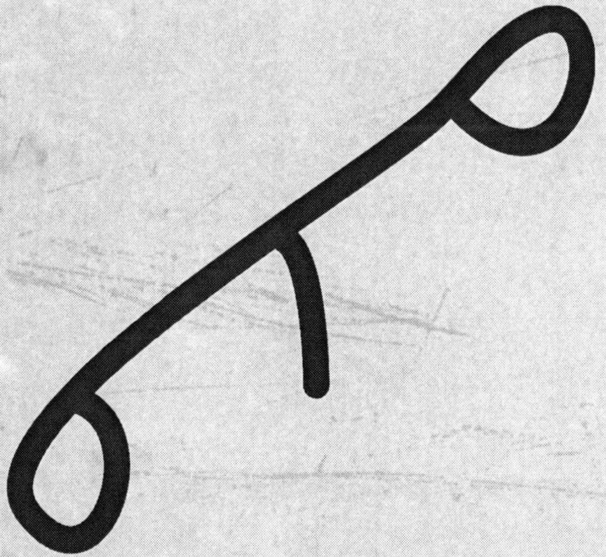

Thursday: **The glyph of Jupiter is**

هرمت

Friday: **The glyph of Venus is**

Saturday: **The glyph of Saturn is**

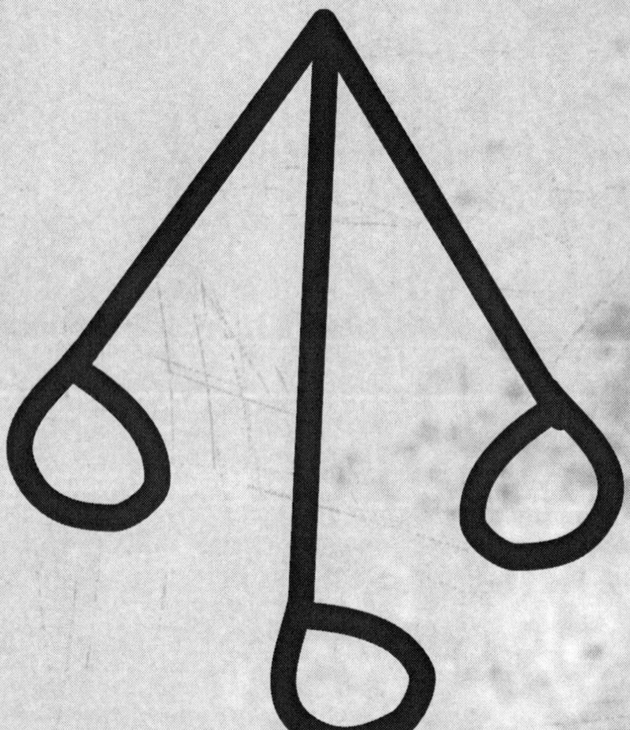

The Glyphs Of The Rites Of The Seven Days

Sunday: رجلا

Monday: لسطلم

Tuesday: لصبرته

Wednesday: سحلوريا

Thursday: شرين شاهيا

Friday: عحح تحلاح طهشيره

Saturday: بصر

Ma'adayus said, "I asked Asaph the son of Berechiah about these glyphs placed on the talismans of the seven days. He said, 'Know that nothing of the sciences is undertaken except with knowledge of the day and its glyph, the ruhani and his glyph, and the planet and its glyph, for inquiry, reproval, casting circles, constructing talismans, or anything else, even for protection and healing. Once you become familiar with that,

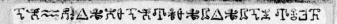

you will come to know its truth.

When you wish to undertake an operation, look at the ascendant and its lord. Draw the glyph between the first and the twelfth of the lunar month, when the moon is free from malefic aspects and in fortunate mansions, aspecting the brilliant planet with a benefic aspect. If it is otherwise, draw it from the twelfth to the twentieth, when the moon is in an unfortunate mansion aspecting Saturn with a square or opposition. If it is for suffering from Winds and pains, draw it during the last part of the month. Know that and the Lord Most High will guide you.'"

By grace, aid, and good success from the Divine, this completes the book.
All Praise is due God alone.
Amen.

Lightning Source UK Ltd.
Milton Keynes UK
UKOW051806311011

181215UK00004B/23/P